Norman Nicholson's Nature

by Ian O. Brodie

written by Ian O. Brodie

ISBN 978-904098-60-07
typeset and processed by Christine Handley

Published by Wildtrack Publishing
Venture House, 103 Arundel Street,
Sheffield S1 2NT

Norman Nicholson

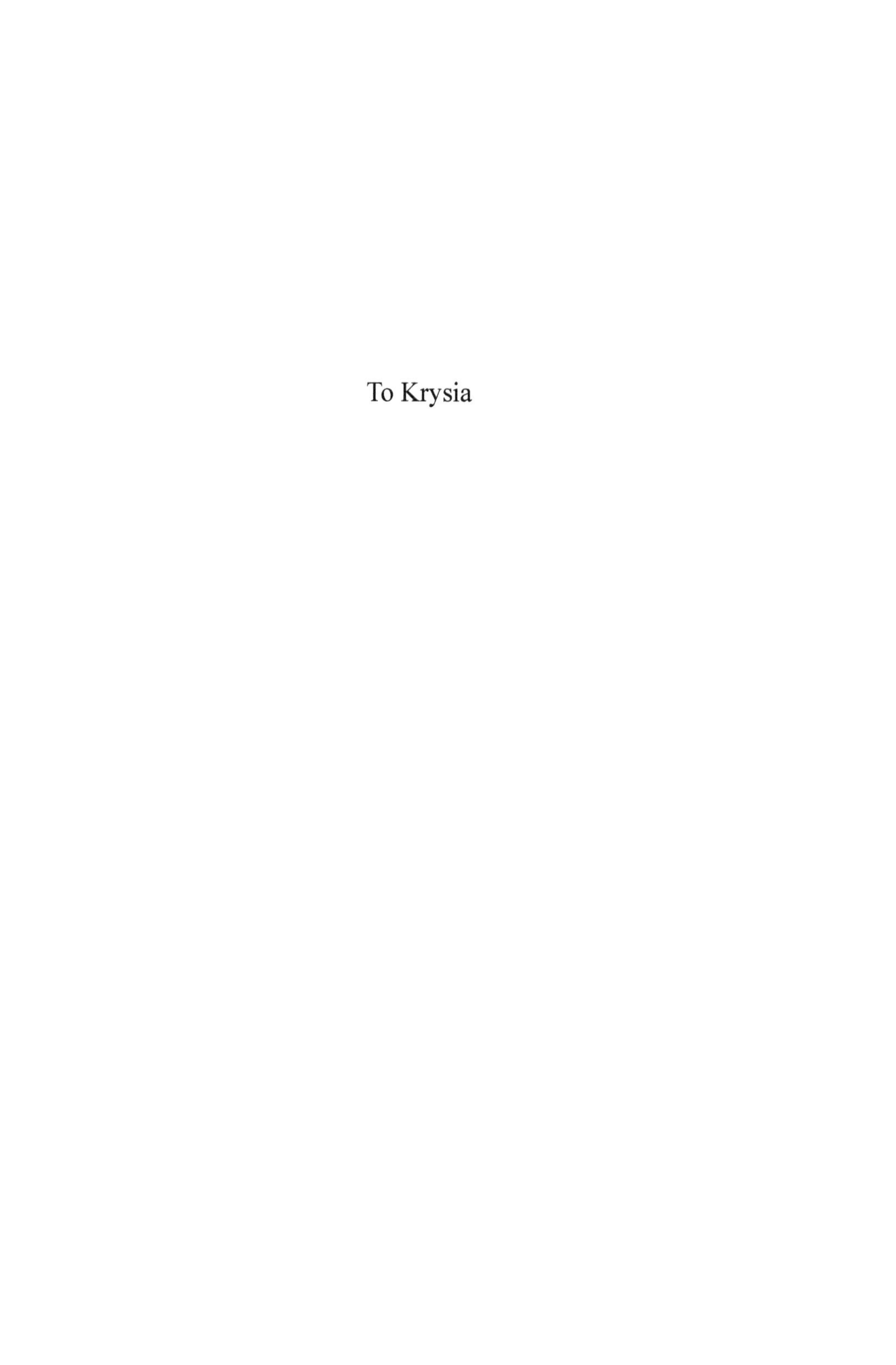

To Krysia

CONTENTS:

Introduction: "Scholar and Priest of Nature" [1]

Millom is a now a post-industrial town that sits uneasily on land which lies on Cumbria's coastal margin, sandwiched between the glorious Duddon Estuary and that huge outlier of the Lake District fells Black Combe. The lower-lying land is underlain by haematite bearing limestone strata which provided the resources for the birth of a mining and iron industry and thus of the town. The closure of the industry almost caused the death of the community. To consider only the bold facts of location of a resource-exploiting town situated adjacent to England's best known landscapes is to ignore the human dimensions of toil, heartache and appreciation of the town's magnificent position. It was here, on 8 January 1914, Norman Cornthwaite Nicholson was born. He died in 1987 as one of the town's more widely known and respected characters, a nationally treasured poet, topographical writer, playwright, lecturer, and broadcaster, though one not without his critics. Apart from a couple of years in a New Forest tuberculosis (TB) sanatorium Norman lived all his life in a terraced house, which as a boy and young adult was his father's outfitters shop, in a corner of old Cumberland that proved the *genius loci* for his life and work.

I use Norman throughout this book respectfully as Nicholson appears too detached. Yes I knew Norman and, along with a few conversations in his house and a few letters we exchanged, he wrote a fore-word for one of my walking books which explored his home acres. (see Appendix 2) But Millom I knew before Norman for, as a youth staying at the school hut high on Coniston Old Man, I would look at night to the belching furnaces of the town spewing their red flame into the dark night some twenty kilometres and 450 metres below our very much cooler eyrie. Like iron, the sight of those furnaces proved, eventually, to be magnetic.

Millom in 1980

Footnotes

(1) *William Wordsworth, an introduction and selection* page xx.

As a child growing up in Millom Norman could not, through the exposure of the town to the elements of climate and weather, have been disconnected from the seasons. He saw the snow on Black Combe and Lakeland fells, the geese moving up or down the estuary and the emergence of flowers on the ore mine heaps. These would all order his sense of natural rhythms. This he clearly demonstrated in the structure and content of his book *Provincial Pleasures* and gives us examples in the more autobiographical *Wednesday Early Closing*.

His first attempt at poetry, whilst at school, described summer as the best of all seasons.[(2)] When exiled in his New Forest tuberculosis sanatorium as a teen his bed and chalet were open to all weathers no matter what the season. Here he experienced the seasons in the raw with their climatic dramas and their wildlife. These formed an indelible 'university of life' experience. We see the seasonal change in his early poems where the end of the old is replaced by the promise of new life:

> [t]hey will see the bracken retard and turn rusty,
> And new fronds like clock-springs coil into gear;
> Many times they will watch the sea's renewal,
> And oftener than we know the renewal of the year. [(3)]

There is, in the poem *Before I was Born*[(4)], an apparent acknowledgement by Norman that his appreciation of Nature and of the values of humanity within Nature came to him later than his upbringing might suggest. Again the time at the TB sanatorium during his teen years is clearly, despite the many hours he spent exploring the local countryside prior to the out-break of the disease, the time of awakening. The poem says the land, which is Norman himself, was dead, thankless, undamned. Nature was represented only by bramble, dog rose, woods, the everyday commonplace that potentially everyone notices. Millom not just buildings but a vital community set within natural habitats. The illusion to Nicodemus signifies his re-birth into a new consciousness awakened by nature. From that time onwards the recognition of place, people, industrial and rural landscapes, and natural history were central to his thinking. The sub-regional landscape was greater than the town of Millom where

Footnotes

(2) *Wednesday Early Closing* page 97.

(3) *Carol for Holy Innocents Day* in *Collected Poems* page 4. Holy Innocents Day is 28 December in the Church of England calendar, a day for the Children's Mass but said to be the unluckiest of the saints days!

(4) *Before I was Born* in *Collected Poems* page 5.

he had lived his sheltered early years. Here he learned of beauty and and that would significantly influence the way he looked at his surroundings.

We find the range of these new awakenings in another early poem *Five Rivers*. [5] Specific places, people at work, geology and geomorphology, landscapes of beauty with their plant and animal components all come together, they might be recognised separately but are treated as part of the great whole. The poem is a physical and geographical exploration of these five Cumbrian rivers - the Ehen, Calder, Irt, Mite and Esk -and a recognition they have varying characters, differing strengths to contribute to Norman's reading of their landscape. His powers of observation were intensified and his future life brought enhanced powers of observation and interpretation of his surroundings. It is not always possible to tease out the separate elements of geology, flora and fauna, landscape, human habitation and Norman's spiritual awareness from his varied output. In the following chapters I try and take these aspects as different elements whilst never forgetting they are only parts of the whole of his awareness and philosophy.

Black Combe in winter.

This philosophy not only is found in his poems and topographical writing but his verse plays and, within his novels.Whilst Norman regarded his novels as the least successful of his work, he cautioned that whilst the characters are fictitious, the topography is 'not entirely imaginary'.[6] Millom, including its people and its industries, are called Odborough in three of Norman's books - *Wednesday Early Closing*, and the two novels, *The Fire of the Lord* and *The Green Shore*. *The Fire of the Lord* is dedicated to the people of the town and all three of these titles reflect the depth of Norman's writings which arose from his meanderings around his natal habitat.

Footnotes

(5) *Five Rivers* in Collected Poems pp. 11-15.

(6) *The Fire of the Lord.*

Like many seasoned observers of the natural landscape Norman could not benefit from his parents or family who had little more than a cursory awareness of the local flora and fauna or of the fells. Indeed his first knowledge of some of the common flowers of the area - Red Campion, Lesser Stitchwort, Germander Speedwell -came from the highly collectable illustrated wild flower cards found in cigarette packets. [(7)]

Thus it was as the teenager leaving behind his boyhood and the close-knit community life of the terraced housing of the built up area that was home when the formative stages of his natural awareness took root. The development of his own acute powers of observation, from the wide vistas of the coast and sky to the very detail at the heart of a single flower, came from his contacts with nature and his great capacity for reading, not least whilst at the TB sanatorium (see below). This ability to see clearly everyday things around him appears to have been a personal learning experience and, if it was not taught in school (there are hints it may have at least helped), it was a skill he so importantly acquired and developed.

The regular wanderings of a boy by the ironworks, along past the haematite mines and along the estuary and coast enabled Norman to explore his home acres. This was not, as with many young people of his age, a physical challenge (he loathed playing most sports) rather more of an experiential amble. The physical surroundings were only part of this because the close-knit community of which he was in regular contact was an integral part of the landscape. One site that proved important to Norman was on the coast at Hodbarrow Point, where the Duddon estuary meets the Irish Sea. This location he specifically mentions in *Wednesday Early Closing* where he quotes the variety of flora he later came to know. Much of this flora can still be found today. It was here around Hodbarrow mines especially that Norman saw where nature had fought back against a declining industrial exploitation of the earth's resources iron ore and limestone.This site set against the elemental open space of the estuary with its relatively untouched-by-man appearance that Norman felt for the first time in his life the meaning of freedom, an escape from the tight community hemmed in by canyons of terraced housing.[(8)] Here was a wide open space where even the overbearing omnipresence of Black Combe receded a little when compared with his home street.

Footnotes

[(7)] *Wednesday Early Closing* p. 122.

[(8)] *Wednesday Early Closing* p. 135.

Hodbarrow Point.

It was in his boyhood, around his eleventh year, that Norman with his father and step-mother, through the benefits of public transport especially the railways, that Norman began to make an increasing number of forays into the Lake District. His step-mother was a keen rambler and perhaps the driving force of these wider explorations. Amongst these forays and of the greater significance, was Norman's first ascent of Black Combe. This Lakeland fell occupies an area of greater square-mileage than any other and its position towards the end of the peninsula gives, on clear days, an unrivalled vista - with Ireland, Scotland, Wales, the Isle of Man and Staffordshire being the maximum extremities. (9)

These outings not only widened the scope of his sense of place but gave him the foundations of a geographical context of his home base. Millom, he soon realised, was part of what he called Greater Lakeland and not an isolated industrial town in the middle of nowhere. With his increasing eye for detail and landform he began to inhabit a wider world for, as a boy, most of his life was centered on the location of his father's shop and his step-mother's strong adherence to the Chapel.

Following his time away in the New Forest, Millom was to be his domicile for the rest of his life. This was not a life to be constrained by a provincial outpost of England but to a place that was the centre of all that mattered to him, a setting in whose special qualities he fully understood and of which he drew inspiration for his literary work. He lived among a human work force employed, when economic conditions allowed, an extractive interface with the local geology, amongst an area of superb natural beauty and which was inhabited by fascinating flora and fauna. Each aspect was part of the whole and we must regard this wide concept of nature as a fundamental inspiration for Norman's work.

Footnotes

(9) See Wordsworth's poem *View from the Top of Black Comb.*

Some people did fortuitously help Norman see this wider picture. His interest in botany, post cigarette card pictures, was catalysed by his new head teacher Walter Wilson, later to be-come a friend for the rest of Wilson's life. Like Wilson, Norman began to explore his local area and note unusual plants and through Wilson's interest and local botanical knowledge fired what was to be a permanent interest for Norman. [(10)]

In the late 1920s, Norman's school pals included Tom Morton (whose black and white photographs were used in Norman's topographical books, but the originals have now proved un-traceable) and under Wilson's influence the two boys walked and cycled the wider hinter-land of Millom. The area covered gradually widened encompassing not only the Black Combe area but as far as Coniston Old Man. This latter fell marks a sad ascent for Norman because, due to the onset of TB shortly afterwards, it appears to have been his last climb, to what was then, the highest point in Lancashire. The nearby and varied landscapes of the Duddon valley, from source to estuary, were also regular haunts for the two explorers. [(11)] So Norman discovered the Lake District, about which he was later to produce some of the best topographical descriptions ever written. He explored the coast, the dales, the woodlands, the bogs, the rivers and long remembered the views from the summits in intimate detail. He had, he said, 'discovered Cumberland' but in reality it was Cumberland, Lancashire and a portion of Westmorland, now Cumbria, that he had investigated. These are grand, often large-scale habitats and landscapes but, through what appears to have been sometimes off-the-beaten track explorations, Norman built up a knowledge of the multiple-facets of a living, working landscape that was to inform his understanding of the area and his work.

The Duddon Valley with Hesk Fell.

Footnotes

(10) *Wednesday Early Closing* p. 139.

(11) *Wednesday Early Closing* pp. 172, 173.

In the autumn of 1930, Norman was exiled from Millom for two years to a TB sanatorium on the edge of the New Forest. His chalet in the grounds was largely open to the weather year round. Birds and other wildlife came into the surrounding gardens and trees and, sometimes, into his chalet. From the adversity of TB, and the subsequent exile, came not only an introduction to a different class of people (his father was digging deeply into his savings to afford the coast of an expensive clinic) but also brought him into close contact with birds. He learned to recognise a variety of birds and took readily to ornithology and with this an understanding of their behaviour and song. Yet he admits that at this time he neglected his nascent interest in botany. (12) However, his often voracious reading at the sanatorium included the writings of naturalists, natural history identification books and rural writers. These enabled him to accumulate a corpus of knowledge and the ability to apply that knowledge to his personal observations. Thus he became an interpreter of nature, of the wildlife he could see and now better understand. It was also towards the end of his stay in the sanatorium that Norman promised himself that he would spend more time in the fresh air of what was to prove an invigorating and inspirational landscape around Millom. (13)

One of Norman's early biographers was an American academic Philip Gardner who suggests Norman's reading of T. S. Eliot opened the poet's eyes to better understanding his local landscape and states

> it stimulated him to look more courageously at his own superficially depressing surroundings.'

Gardner then quoted Norman,

> 'It was Mr. Eliot...who made us aware of the meadow behind the muckheap, who pointed out the significance of the dilapidated school and the empty church on the hill. It was not a very hopeful picture that he made of it, but at twenty years of age, we did not both much but hope ... indeed, we found despair quite exhilarating. What mattered was that suddenly everything in our world had its meaning. The most disparate events and objects took on a new relation to each other, becoming allegorical while remaining themselves.'

Footnotes

(12) *Wednesday Early Closing* p. 190.

(13) *Wednesday Early Closing* p. 200.

Gardner then adds a most significant paragraph

> [t]he ability to relate "disparate objects" was further encouraged by Nicholson's interest in wild flowers. At first he studied these in "natural" surroundings of a conventional rural sort; but to find the rarer species he had to hunt among the abandoned workings of the iron-ore mines. This search drew his eye back to the town, and he came to realize that it, too, was a part of nature: "I saw that the black-headed gulls nested just as happily among the slagbanks and old rubble tips as they did on the sand-dunes at Ravenglass, and if the incongruity of the site did not bother them, why should it bother me? (14)

Gardner at least recognises, even if he did not discuss more fully, that 'the connection of man with nature, and of the man in past and present dimensions - are central to a proper understanding of Norman Nicholson's poetry.

Norman's use of natural examples was not wholly consistent in his poetic output. Poems on specific types of plant or animal, such as a *Black Guillemot* or *Bee Orchid at Hodbarrow*, only formed a small proportion of his output. Most of these are found in earlier works but at its peak with the volume of poems, *Sea to the West*, published in 1981. More often the comparison of a flower or rock or animal is used directly or as a metaphor, for example we are invited to see a rock surface as *smooth as walnut*, but there were periods where we see less of this approach to his writing. *Sea to the West* is more personal than most and reflects on his life lived in an industrial town. Millom by this time was struggling to find reasons for its economic existence. But the town remained surrounded by a still vital, living landscape but one in which Norman's ability to access had become physically constrained. This relationship indicates a higher realm of the personal sustenance he gained from the whole of this variegated landscape character increasingly feeding into and defining his sense of place, his *genius loci*, within this home acre. He realised just how rich Millom and its environs were in geography, geology, history, wildlife, beautiful landscapes and human stories.

Various sources reflect on Norman's connection with William Wordsworth and the Romantic period. Some found it difficult to see that Robert Southey, S. T. Coleridge and William Wordsworth could be challenged as the Lake District poets. Certainly, in terms of his approach to Nature, Norman was

Footnotes

(14) *Norman Nicholson* by Philip Gardner, pp. 21 & 24 - 25.

well schooled in the Romantic tradition but that does not make him, as critics appear to have alleged, a pale imitator of Wordsworth. In fact Norman was critical of much of Wordsworth's work (especially some of his more popular output) despite holding him in the highest esteem amongst English poets (but not as great as Milton). (15) Norman found common ground with Wordsworth in acknowledging they both probably had inherited Norse genes! (16) More telling than his introduction are the selections Norman made of Wordsworth's poetry. He filed the selected poems under six headings yet, not unexpectedly given Wordsworth's output, some may argue all these poems with perhaps three exceptions (17) share the same context and themes as Norman. These being geographical location, elemental, floral or faunal nature, and some with an allegorical or metaphorical connection with nature. Both were keen botanists although Norman would not accept that adjective, he said he saw plants only as wild flowers. Naturally Wordsworth's work focusing on Black Combe and the Duddon feature in the selection. These intimate but extensive geographical areas proved seminal for both writers. Wordsworth was taken, in one of his two poems that feature the fell, with the size and extent of view from the summit of Black Combe. His Duddon Sonnets culminate with a desire to explore the Duddon estuary. For Norman there were his home ground and feature in a significant proportion of his work, if not directly then inspirationally.

Black Combe.

Given the huge influence nature and place had on Wordsworth it might be argued that few of his poems would ignore such features that also proved fundamental to Norman's life. However, it might also be worthwhile to think about how Norman's topographical writings mirror Wordsworth' seminal Guide to the Lakes. In both authors we can see that nature encompasses human ecology

Footnotes

(15) See Norman's views on Wordsworth in his introduction to *William Wordsworth, an introduction and selection.*

(16) *William Wordsworth, an introduction and selection* p.ix

(17) These three are *She was a Phantom of Delight* (page 105); *On the Extinction of the Venetian Republic* (p. 125); and *Inside of King's College Chapel, Cambridge* (p. 127).

and people cannot be assumed to be separate or, as some would have, above nature. This fundamental is what much of the following chapters consider. Thus the fundamentals of the Romanticism are key to understanding Norman as a poet of Nature, what Norman calls Wordsworth's 'early feeling for nature, and the religion of the heart'. He adds, later, 'Once, indeed, he had true innocence and true communion with nature, [...]'. [(18)] With Norman his view of a young Wordsworth was to permeate his thoughts throughout his life. Norman said of Wordsworth that he encompassed 'the acceptance of the entire beauty of the created world, of the essential rightness and righteousness of matter.' [(19)] and such words may be appropriately turned to apply to Norman.

Norman was certainly a person to have opinions about the effect people had, and were still having, on the landscape. These views are expressed most trenchantly in his topographical books and, at times, he took a different opinion to those of the conservation bodies he had joined. Consequently he had views about his understanding of the preservation of the landscape, especially on matters of forestry and reservoirs in the Lake District National Park, which had been designated in 1951. Whilst his opinions are relevant to understanding his work they are not necessarily fundamental to asking how Norman's work might be relevant today. When we read his work it is sometimes difficult to remember that the decades of his largest amount of topographical work, published from 1949 to 1969 but mostly researched and written in the 1940s and 1950s with some necessary updating in the 1960s, was a time when an understanding of the issues he raised was vastly different to that today. We understand more now about the nuclear, forestry, water resource and tourism concerns, for example, which he constantly and in an original and pioneering way, raised. Consequently we have to regard his opinions as being from an era long-gone and we have now moved an enormous distance in respect of understanding their consequences. We should therefore, be more interested in how Norman saw the relationship between people and nature in an holistic sense than in his contemporary view of specific issues.

There are, in other works on Norman a recognition of him being a poet of nature but relatively few when compared with commentaries on other aspects of Norman's writings. But regarding Norman has a nature writer has, in the view of the author, been too little and too inconsistent. Whilst not all published commentaries have been cited in this book it was more the trend, certainly in

Footnotes

(18) *William Wordsworth, an introduction and selection* p. xx.

(19) *William Wordsworth, an introduction and selection* p. xxiii.

earlier publications, to concentrate on the provincial or the Christian readings of Norman's work.

Philip Gardner, the American academic, in his 1973 critical analysis of Norman's work, is rather blunt when he states in his opening paragraph

> during the last twenty-five years or so a body of poetry whose close combination of Christian belief and regional subject matter can reasonably be described as unique in contemporary British literature. [20]

He called these his twin concerns 'region and religion' [21] but Gardner only permits himself minimal attention, in his understanding of the region, an area which encompasses Norman's wider natural interests. Gardner regards Norman's other work as 'peripheral'.[22] This author does allow a few pages to set the context for what he calls '*The Poet's Landscape*' and this comprises a brief and accurate outline of the Millom and surrounding areas but acknowledges

> the region is also one of considerable beauty. It has not only the elemental natural beauty of sea cliffs, green turf edging its little frequented shore, varicoloured mountain slopes rising inland ...but also the beauty produced by the long human associations of the landscape. The area is, in effect, a palimpsest of history, a microcosm of human evolution and development.[23]

Gardner then turned his description to Millom and its industry. Few other reviewers of Norman's work have noted his natural and pioneering ecological concerns.

Gardner's critical and analytic work recognised some value in nature to Norman but he rarely brought this vital aspect into his book, he was too focused on Norman's Christianity and his location in Millom away from the London-centric world of poetry. In the rare exceptions to this general statement he does spend time looking at the poet's geological interests but rather too readily dismisses this as 'rocks are to be regarded as permanent and thus equate with God.'

Footnotes

(20) *Norman Nicholson* by Philip Gardner, Preface paragraph 1.
(21) *Norman Nicholson* by Philip Gardner, Preface paragraph 4.
(22) *Norman Nicholson* by Philip Gardner, Preface paragraph 4.
(23) *Norman Nicholson* by Philip Gardner, Preface, pp 16-21.

Millom and a cloud covered Black Combe from Hodbarrow, May 2013

It would be misplaced to assume in what follows that Norman's Christianity has been ignored. Rather the opposite, for the way he developed his understanding of the natural and human landscapes in which he lived not only underpinned his spirituality but gave him foundations on which to rebuild his faith following his times of doubt. Norman once admitted he was, when as a young regular chapel attender in his twenties, 'a near atheist'.[24]

His output was not always consistently nature-oriented for, after reading Robert Lowell's *Life Studies* his writings became more human in their content.[25] But to Norman people are an integral part of nature and thus human ecology is an essential component, a co-naturality, of our more general but misleading understanding of the use of the expression nature.

It is not my primary purpose to look at Norman's life nor to comment critically on his corpus of work for these have been more thoroughly covered in other books about him.[26] Rather my main purpose is to suggest, whilst accepting the volume of his work can benefit from further critical reading or re-appraisal, he has been, correctly but too insistently, branded as a regional and a christian poet. My contention is he was, as many of his readers readily understand, essentially a poet and writer of nature, but not to the exclusion of his spirituality or of the personal content of his work. His naming as a provincial or regional

Footnotes

[24] *Wednesday Early Closing* p. 93.

[25] See Curry in his introduction to *Collected Poems* p. xxi.

[26] See *Norman Nicholson* by Philip Gardner, Twayne, New York, 1973; *Norman Nicholson - Collected Poems* edited and introduced by Neil Curry, Faber & Faber, London, 1984; *Norman Nicholson* by Neil Curry, Northern Lights, Carlisle, 2001; *Norman Nicholson The Whispering Poet* by Kathleen Jones, Appleby, 2013.

poet (a term of derision which Norman learned to treat as a badge of honour) is further demolished by being a person who could relate to the whole of nature. As such the need to introduce his work to a wider audience, as he wanted, is fully recognised. As a teen Norman discovered both nature and, also as a chapel- and church-goer, that life has a spiritual dimension. These attributes he retained throughout the his life and, for a significant part of this time, he was a committed Christian. On his death The Times obituary branded him, too simply, as 'the most gifted English Christian poet of his century.' [(27)] These aspects of his persona were underpinned by his view that nature both physically surrounded and touched him deeply. His understanding was that nature was wider than the elemental wildness he found on the coast, in the fells, in the climate, and in the geology of his home area. To Norman nature included wildlife and, equally, human life. He may, for significant parts of his life, have viewed these aspects as God's creations but without his depth of response to his surroundings and their range of contexts and interconnectedness his spiritual outlook on life, and thus his religion, would have been without substance. Much of Norman's written work relied heavily on his experiences of nature.

ACKNOWLEDGMENTS

Throughout the book I have referred to the *Collected Poems* as the source of the poetic references as this is currently the most convenient way to access all the material however, in preparing the book, I have worked with the original published volumes as listed in Appendix 1. I am grateful to the Millom Discovery Centre for their enthusiasm and for their willingness to allow the use of their picture collection. For visitors to Millom this centre is a vital first port of call and they have published a useful book of local walks. I am also hugely grateful for the time and advice of Esther Rutter and Christine Handley. My thanks also go to Irvine Hunt and the David Higham Associates.

Footnotes

[(27)] *Collected Poems* - Neil Curry's introduction page xv.

Wasdale Screes

Chapter 1: Geology and Geomorphology: *As a stone, simple as a sample of mountain* [1]

We are not told directly in *Wednesday Early Closing* when or where Norman's infatuation with geology began. However, the clues are there on almost every page of the book as Norman was an acute observer of the physical materials which surrounded him. Throughout his life when the breathing difficulties resulting from his tuberculosis (TB) allowed, he explored the fells, dales and, most particularly, the town and the seashore of his native Cumberland and the adjoining Lancashire coast.[2] As Ruskin believed, the training of an artist provided the skills to look closely and carefully at the full picture so Norman applied his strong observational eyes and his analytic and imaginative mind to the rocks of the landscape.

A spring of the nascent river Duddon gives an image of the detail he was acutely able to observe:

> [...] from your source
> There when you bubble through the moss on Wrynose
> (Among the ribs of bald and bony fells
> With scree scratches in the turf like grey scabs).[3]

His geological science was in some ways superficial. He had a clear understanding of the basic geology and geomorphological processes which had shaped the landscapes he experienced, but without the depth of technical detail that would have earned him recognition as an amateur geologist. What he did know about these earth sciences he understood well and, as we find in his topographical books, especially *Cumberland and Westmorland*, he was able to convey this knowledge in a fresh and engaging manner. He describes the Wasdale screes of Illgill Head as 'the whole slope stands in fluted tapering columns shaped very much like the fan-vaulting of a cathedral turned upside down.'[4] This description gives you an immediate word picture of the geological landscape.

Footnotes

(1) *Silecroft Shore* Collected Poems pp. 170 – 175.

(2) Prior to the re-organisation of local government and the formation of the administrative county of Cumbria, in April 1974, west of the River Duddon was Cumberland and, to the east, Lancashire. The Furness area of Lancashire, Cumberland and Westmorland, along with three parishes from the former West Riding of Yorkshire became the new county of Cumbria. In earlier times the river formed the boundary of the Scottish kingdom of Strathclyde.

(3) *To the River Duddon* Collected Poems p. 24.

(4) *Cumberland and Westmorland* p. 20.

Mining is frequently Norman's way into geology with Millom having, during his lifetime, a rich iron ore (haematite) mine at Hodbarrow. Rocks give ores and ores provide resources which humans exploit and thus for Norman there is a continuous, natural connection between rocks and people's lives. As a boy and teenager, as in later life, Norman used to walk amongst the haematite mine and subsequent abandoned site. Along with the area's rocks used in local house construction, these were probably the key to understanding his earliest geological insights. This probably gave him the encouragement to recognise the relationships between different types of rock and the varied landscapes and economic processes that he found around his home habitat.

Geology was so deeply engrained in Norman's mind that it can become the foundation for us to understand a huge portion of his work - be it poetry, topographical, fiction, verse plays or his religious writings. In 1964 a booklet was published of the six short talks he gave for the BBC. In his Foreword to this booklet the Bishop of Manchester describes them as 'sermons in stone' but also provides us with a key understanding of Norman when he noted 'We see here a poet and a lover of the countryside pondering how the spiritual order mirrors itself in the natural order.'[(5)] Norman had, earlier, written

> [p]erhaps in no other part of England has the life and character of a district and its people been so controlled by the nature of the rock and by the forces which have acted upon it. In Cumberland and Westmor land the rock is indeed the land.[(6)]

Norman gave his reasons for being interested in the fells as they are 'bare, unpopulated, uncultivated parts of the earth's surface, you can see our physical environment reduced to its simplest terms: rock, water and air.'[(7)] He goes on to recognise that physical change does occur in the hills - especially through the slow erosion of geological processes - heat, ice, rain and streams that scrub and scour and grind the rocks down. He noted elsewhere, as he did in the talks,

> [b]ecause of the immense ages of what we might call geological time we are inclined to think that the formative forces belong to the past. But except for the ice they are still at work today - frost, sun, wind, rain, rivers. The landscape, in fact, is changing before our eyes and more rapidly, perhaps, than we think.[(8)]

Footnotes

(5) *Enjoying It All* p. 3.
(6) *Cumberland and Westmorland* p. 10.
(7) *Enjoying It All* p. 5.
(8) *Cumberland and Westmorland* p. 48.

Each talk - The Hills; The Seaside; The Country Towns; The Seasons; The Working Towns; and The Pattern of Life are homilies based on geology, geomorphology and the other natural aspects of the earth and their relationship to the whole of Nature and to their consistent, inclusive spirituality.

His description of volcanic activity not only permeates his topographical works but also his autobiographical texts

> [t]hen in a jiffy of millennia the sea begins to simmer. Volcanoes break out like carbuncles. A red-hot pus of lava bursts through the underskin of the ocean, and the vapour stinks and fumes, boiling in tidal waves against the coasts. Under-sea deluges of ash stain the water black in a sewer where the cooled lava creates a new slag-like land scape. Slowly under the scrubbing and bludgeoning of the tide, lava and ash, in their turn, consolidate to rock, [...][9]

Norman continued with descriptions of more recent geological epochs and the rocks that formed and which underlie (and roof over) his life and that of the community of Millom. The product of this activity was also given a fertile and

Millom stone built housing pictured in 1980.

Footnotes

(9) *Cumberland and Westmorland* p. 15.

inspirational description

> [t]he volcanic rocks are contorted and fantastic, like creatures of folklore, but the Skiddaw fells are like prehistoric monsters, still sleeping through the millennia of the rock, and sometimes not seeming to sleep.(10)

Much of the local coastal geology is comprised of limestone and sandstone - rocks of sedimentary origin and therefore potential sites for fossils. In his *Fossils* poem Norman recognised the fossil types and the dynamic cycle of way the sea erodes them back into grains and then into re-cycled minerals that one day may again be part of living nature and potential future fossils.

> In the bones of the rock
> The fossils are living,
> Crinoid and ammonite;
> In the red of the rock
> (sandstone and haematite)
> The fossils are moving,
> Coiling, crawling,
> Aching for the sea.(11)

In one of his major poems,*The Seven Rocks*, Norman takes his theme from the seven major rock types found in his home area and the wider Lake District and allocated to each rock one of the seven cardinal Christian virtues. The rocks he placed in order of age so we find the Skiddaw Slates, the underlying rock of Black Combe, allegorically serves as faith, Scafell Ash as hope, Coniston Flag as Charity, Eskdale Granite as Fortitude, Mountain limestone as Prudence, Maryport Coal as Justice, and the last in his order, St. Bees Sandstone, as temperance. Whilst this Christian connection is strong we have to be equally impressed with the way Norman relates the character of the landscape to the nature of the underlying strata. For example in Eskdale Granite 'The Granite pate breaks bare to the sky'. In other verses we learn about the origins of the specific rock as in Mountain Limestone (Carboniferous Limestone) where 'Out of the shells the sea-beasts creep.[…]'. Maryport Coal (Upper Carboniferous) was formed from 'The fountains of plunging ferns[…]'.(12) This poem is fundamental to the reading of a whole range of Norman's work not least his topographical accounts of his home region.

Footnotes

(10) *Provincial Pleasures* p. 19.

(11) *Fossils* Collected Poems pp. 216 - 217.

(12) *The Seven Rocks* Collected Poems pp. 242 - 251.

When William Wordsworth wrote his '*Guide to the Lake District*' (first published in 1810) he was fully aware of the relationship between landscape and the underlying rocks and to the work of ice and water in eroding that landscape. In the 1835 edition, Wordsworth persuaded his friend Professor Adam Sedgwick (born in Dent in the Yorkshire Dales) to contribute three letters on geology. In the next edition, of 1842, this was increased to five letters. Sedgwick was the first British professor of geology and, at the time of the establishment of this new science, one of its major pioneers. When Norman wrote most of his topographical work, a century or so later, the science had moved on considerably and thus the understanding of rocks and geological processes was greatly heightened - as it has again been since Norman's books were published. In his introduction to his selection of Wordsworth's poems Norman cannot resist introducing a geological context and metaphor. He argues the limestone and sandstone rocks shaped the lives of people with whom Wordsworth had an early relationship. Yet he disparages, unfairly, the lack of influence these rocks, when compared with the older rocks of the more upland area of the Lake District, had on Wordsworth's poetic output. He attributes these older geological formations as the more seminal influence for much of the Grasmere poet's work, a choice Norman maintained was 'very deliberate.'[13] Norman argues that, as Wordsworth's formative years were spent away from the Lake District, 'so that I shall not be accused of saying that his work was a direct product of the rock; nevertheless the rock provides an interesting analogy of his poetic development.'[14] Wordsworth had a few years at university (from 1787) and spent some time on the continent but most of his early years were in the Lake District (1779 to 1787 he was at school in Hawkshead). This makes Norman's charge a little false. After a further paragraph of Lakeland geology Norman adds:

> Wordsworth had little interest in geology - and indeed he satirizes (...) the geologist in The Excursion, though, later, he asked Professor Sedgwick to contribute letters on the geology of the Lake District to his Guide - but he certainly had a feeling for rock.[15]

Given the very early development of geology at the beginning of the early nineteenth-century, Norman's criticism is perhaps over strong. However, the point is that Norman was drawing a distinction between Wordsworth and him-

Footnotes

(13) *William Wordsworth - An Introduction and a Selection* p. xi.

(14) *William Wordsworth* p. xiii.

(15) *William Wordsworth* p. xiii.

self, that Norman better understood geology and geological process, that he had developed a greater interest and grasp of the science and he was telling us that, without understanding something of this ourselves, we as readers would never fully appreciate Norman's output. We can therefore perhaps ignore Norman's attempt to equate three main rocks of central Lakeland (Skiddaw Slates, Borrowdale Volcanic and the Silurian, the latter now called Windermere Supergroup) with what he called Wordsworth's 'three modes of poetry' where, for example,'the volcanic rock represents the soaring poetry of Tintern Abbey'. [16]

Wasdale - a Borrowdale Volcanic landscape.

Like many topographical writers in the second half of the twentieth-century, not least those in the ground-breaking New Naturalists series, Norman's opening description of place often begin with a chapter to establish the geology and geomorphology of the area. But, for Norman, this was not just standard practice, rather that rocks were the foundation of all his thinking and the very

Footnotes

[16] *William Wordsworth* p. xiii.

essences of much of his metaphorical references. This is evident not just in the poem *The Seven Rocks* and others but in his plays and in his broadcast talks recorded in the booklet *Enjoying It All*:

> That is how this universe works. The breaking down of one rock leads to the building up of another; the giving up of one life leads to the building up of another. Birth and death, taking and giving, pleasure and pain, are all part of the process by which everything in this world is kept going.[17]

So rock types represent not only the character of the landscape but underpin the natural habitats, the areas of human habitation and the economic functions of the community, and are fundamental to the human psyche. We see this through this one poem *The Seven Rocks*, from the formation of the rock, to each rock's contribution to the landscape, through economic activity and, the interaction with the weather and climate, the nature of the underlying strata determines the nature of life, human and natural. This work is one of Norman's most seminal writings, one of his most holistic and one that underlines his philosophy that, notwithstanding the human interactions with the natural landscape and with the elemental rocks, we are mere mortals who must recognise our place as only a part of nature and not the dominant force on earth. Whilst the rocks represented the seven virtues of Christian morality (three theological and four cardinal virtues) for Norman the virtues themselves became an analogy for the rocks, 'an attempt in specific human terms some qualities which I found in the rocks themselves.' [18] Additionally rocks remain a source of inspiration:

> To look at the scenery of Cumberland and Westmorland without trying to understand the rock is like listening to poetry in an unknown language - you hear the beauty of the sounds but you miss the meaning.[19]

Norman concluded his chapter on the rocks of Cumbria stating that whilst the rocks give character to the landscape 'they do not of themselves give it personality. For this it needed a shaping influence, like a person needs to rub up against other people.'[20] The natural shaping influence was largely ice and

Footnotes

(17) *Enjoying it All* p. 8.

(18) The Nicholson quote is taken from *Norman Nicholson* by Neil Curry p. 13.

(19) *Cumberland and Westmorland* p. 40.

(20) *Cumberland and Westmorland* p. 10.

water. The recognition Norman gave to the way rocks had influenced human life, economic activity -from mining and quarrying to agriculture, and the way their chemistry affects the growth of plants was a major part of his belief that without the interaction of a dynamic human and natural ecology the rocks would only remain as unseen and under-valued foundations to life. It was a recognition that landscape is a living dynamic concept of which rocks are only an integral part.

THE CHANGING LANDSCAPE

The way the rocks are affected by natural forces, what are described as geo-morphology, is to be found throughout Norman's work and was first found in early poems such as *Corregidor* where the attrition of the Pacific Ocean's tides serves as a metaphor for the expanding tentacles of a world war;

> Like the Pacific, pounding on the shore,
> Like the shingle shovelled and hurled at the bare
> Cliff, like the buffet and blow and shock
> Of the heavy fist of the sea on the rock.(21)

The Duddon estuary is remarkable for the dramatic effect it has on the land-scape and on human communication. It is a surrogate Millom-by-the-sea as much for some residents as the west coast resorts of Silecroft or Seascale provide more direct access to the Irish Sea. It has, compared with other north-western estuaries, a large proportion of sand exposed at low tide rather than mud. This geomorphological reflection did not escape Norman where he describes, in a novel, 'The Sandbank lay grey and glinting...'.(22) This estu-ary provides the most dominant geomorphological influence in the area and for Norman even the fringing saltmarsh was explored physically and in his mind and, in what is an area of little consequence for most people, explored as a specific habitat deserving attention in its own right. This land sometimes subject to high-tidal inundation of a saline wash and here you might observe plants 'sea-plantain or scurvy grass or maybe Dutch rush, washed by the seep-age of the tide.' (23) The estuary serves as a context, an inspiration and a meta-phor for Norman where we find a tide that ebbed and flowed as much in the

Footnotes

(21) *Corregidor* Collected Poems page 3. Corregidor is a Pacific Island near Manila and was the site of a major World War II battle in May, 1942.

(22) *The Fire of the Lord* p. 50.

(23) *Provincial Pleasures* p. 15.

lives of the people of Millom. Norman expressed this in writing from his attic bedroom in St. George's Terrace:

> Here - among the chimney pots and aerials, I feel the weight of the tides of the Ordovician Age - slow estuarine tides in which mud sank and settled to form the rock which is now heaped in a hill above the town.[24]

Duddon Sands.

The Duddon tides were integral to Norman's nature and internal calendars, almost a timepiece for his daily life 'Daily I feel the tug of the tide in my blood.' [25]

The tidal flow was well observed before Norman uses it as a metaphor:

> It is not so much that the tide goes out as that the sands come in. For half an hour or more after the time of high tide the water seemed to be hesitating, slipping back and then edging up again. [26]

Anyone who has spent time on the tidal edge of an estuary will recognise this dynamic interplay between earth and water and, just as the tide threatens to overlap your stance, the land again begins to emerge from the water.

Footnotes

(24) *Provincial Pleasures* p. 19. The fell referred to is Black Combe and which I reflect in the final chapter.

(25) *Maiden's Song* Collected Poems p. 35.

(26) *Provincial Pleasures* p. 152.

During World War II the Duddon Sands were used for aerial bombing practice and it is Norman's setting of the scene for such an activity that stands out - the estuary calm at high tide:

> In the long estuary now the water
> At the top and turn of the tide
> Is quiet as a mountain tarn,
> Smooth and dull as pewter,
> Pale as the mauve sea-aster
> In the turf of the gutter-side. (27)

The poem *The Bow in the Clouds* begins with a vivid, experiential description of the sun on the low-tide sands of the estuary. The pattern of sand surface is never planar but waved and shaped by natural processes - a keenly observed geomorphological process, that in turn, mirrors the myriad changes in reflected light. This poem sets the foundation for what is arguably Norman's most mystical poem.(28)

Crossing the sands of the Duddon is no longer a frequent an event as it was before the construction of the railway from Barrow to Millom. Crossing the sands of Morecambe Bay, the Kent Sands with guide Cedric Robinson and, to a lesser extent, the crossing of the Leven Sands are still large-scale events with several hundred people turning out for most walks. Yet, prior to the railway construction, crossing the Duddon was not only the shortest route but a major highway from the south to Scotland. Norman knew his history well and recorded this (29) yet was always loathe to get his own feet wet at the seaside. That did not stop him combining the lore, geomorphology, natural history and tidal processes, all linked to the interplay of light on the sands at various stages of the tide. This place was often the focus of the best of his imaginative and spiritual writing. Whilst he knew the west-Cumberland shoreline most intimately, he also ventured along the eastern, Lancashire shore as his poems and writings about Askam (30) and Barrow testify. The depth of his understand-

Footnotes

(26) *Provincial Pleasures* p. 152.
(27) *Bombing Practice* Collected Poems p. 28.
(28) *The Bow in the Clouds* Collected Poems pp. 103 - 111.
(29) *Provincial Pleasures* pp. 142 - 143.
(30) *Provincial Pleasures* p. 7.

The Duddon Sands and Black Combe.

ing can be seen, for example, when he writes the 'channel that admits the tide into a small creek where sea-lavender grows.'[(31)]

Throughout his life and career Norman constantly returned to the shore and the Duddon estuary though, as already noted, he was not a person to get his feet wet. The surface of the estuary or beach - sand, mud, shingle, saltmarsh, mosses - were the stages for the interactions of people and wildlife, the places where:

> The wild geese
> Feed beneath the mist, grey and still as sheep' by
> 'The world of field and farm, the woods and the embankment.[(32)]

Norman always found this a place of inspiration - the changing light and tides and season always producing some new effect for the eye and the ear. This fascination did apparently tempt him to make a crossing of the often ill-defined line between firm saltmarsh and less well-defined soft mud as it was a crossing point for the increasingly blurred boundary from the domicile of people to that of Nature. The boundary, as the reality, is ill-defined, the shore and the sands are part of the same continuum of an estuary.

Geomorphological change is effected, over time, by the climatic elements and Millom, being set below Black Combe on an exposed low-lying peninsula,

Footnotes

(31) The place is Salthouse Pool. *Provincial Pleasures* p. 143.

(32) *Across the Estuary* Collected Poems pp. 166-169.

is a place where the weather is difficult to ignore. Weather forms a persistent theme in much of Norman's writings. Rain, for example, can be found at its most beneficient on a 'warm, moist, muzzy night' when it is 'not so much falling as floating, drifting, even streaming upwards'.[33] It is, however, the greater extremes of rain, wind, ice and snow that are more frequently brought to the focus of our attention. Life was lived to the calendar of the elements and, on a twice-daily basis, the movements of the tides. Whilst Norman was acutely aware of the millennia-long time-depth relationship of the rocks and geomorphological processes he was also aware of how elemental weather can also work on the land and people in a shorter time-span. He compares, for example, the effects of a hard winter on the Lake District landscape as it mirrors, in miniature, the glacial process of the last Ice-Age, an epoch that gave the landscape with which he was familiar its basic shape and pattern. In *The Land Under the Ice* we find a description of the seasonal effects of a winter climate on the fells physically. Here Norman shows the effects on the agricultural cycles, especially on the fell sheep farming, and with an in-depth understanding of the influence of an arctic effect on residual arctic-alpine flora of the Lakeland fells. Whilst it is cogently argued that there is no part of England where the landscape has not been altered to some degree by the economic activities of people there is in Norman's poems and topographical writing a stark reminder that we should never underestimate the climate and resulting weather acting as a raw, elemental force and about which we cannot fail to respect how nature can dominate our lives. The poem *The Land Under the Ice* appeared in a volume entitled *Rock Face* and much of the work in this collection helps the reader to reflect on how Norman recognised nature as a still dominant force in people's lives.[34]

Although Norman would never claim to approach his work scientifically, we find in the poem *Beck* his most objective reflection of geomorphological processes of erosion by a stream on the landscape. Not only do we find a detailed analysis but, as in much of Norman's output, we are conscious of a time-depth dimension, as a regard for the landscape change beyond the natural span of flora or fauna or a human life.[35] This recognition that the earth and its natural processes are not only millennia old but will continue beyond the lives of people again can help us to see our place in the context of these geological timescales. Our finite lives are short compared with the timescales of the natu-

Footnotes

[33] *Askam Unvisited* and *Askam Visited* for example Collected Poems pp. 37 - 40.

[34] *The Land Under the Ice* Collected Poems pp. 116 -121.

[35] *Beck* Collected Poems pp. 319-320.

Great Gable in winter.

ral world and can assist us to orientate our lives towards finding our place in nature. This is confirmed in some of his later work, especially his Norwegian poems which not only confirm Norman's life-long fascination with geomorphological processes but his continued recognition of our place in the whole.[36]

Other places where he contemplated such eon-long change were in his broadcast talks, where the small stones on the beach were still recognizable as pieces of rock. He notes,'The geological process hasn't finished with them, they are still receiving the water-treatment.' and adds, [w]hich indeed, is how all the mountains are going to end up - as sand or dust or soil. And that is how most of them began [...]. [37] So this gradual erosion process 'is not an end, but a beginning. I know I've been talking about the destructive power of running water, but I might just as well have been talking about its creative power.'[38]

Change can be seen as either corrosive or constructive and that is a matter which is addressed in more detail in later chapters.

Footnotes

(36) See *Fjord, Glacier*, and *Landing on Staffa* from Collected Poems pp. 352 - 353; 350 - 351 and 355 - 357 respectively.

(37) *Enjoying It All* p. 7.

(38) *Enjoying It All* p. 8.

Chapter 2: Industrial Landscape: "Crags of Slag, Acres of Brick " [1]

When we talk about nature and natural beauty we almost invariably search our minds for images of flora and fauna or of semi-wild landscapes. Yet this narrow interpretation of nature was never envisaged by the earlier Romantic writers of which Norman was a descendent. Wordsworth refers to native beauty in his Guide to the Lakes [2] a phrase which, following the battle between the Thirlmere Defence Association and Manchester City Council over the soul and physical appearance of Thirlmere, became officially transformed to natural beauty.[3] Almost up to the end of the Second World War there was little distinction made between natural history, landscape and the sustainable use of the earth's resources, all were part of nature and, as Norman inherited from the Romantics, humankind was regarded as part of nature and not a separate, more dominant, force.

Such an approach would have been consistent with Norman's education, not least his reading and the influence of his teacher Walter Wilson, perhaps from his Methodist Chapel association in his early days, but less so from his attendance at the more muscular Church of England. His understanding of the dangers and sweat of men mining haematite and then blasting the ore into iron, or the miners from north-Cumberland exploiting the seams of coal and iron ore, were part of the human relationship with rocks and thus with nature. But technologies were changing over time, and with them the economics of the industries with which he was familiar. These changes brought hardships to families but, as Norman rarely admitted, could devastate the landscape. Above that, he was sure, once industry had closed and the workers departed, nature would find a place amongst the waste-heaps and slag-banks of industry.

The mining towns of Cleator Moor, Whitehaven, Askam-in-Furness are all accorded recognition in poems; towns were industry and communities were simply part of the overall scheme of nature. In two earlier poems, *Cleator Moor* [4] and *Whitehaven* [5] we find references to natural history integral to the industrial setting. In the first it is to berries and the latter to curlews and seaweed

Footnotes

(1) *The Tune the Old Cow Died Of* Collected Poems pp. 293 - 294.

(2) *Guide to the Lakes* William Wordsworth p. 83.

(3) See Brodie, I. *Thirlmere and the Birth of the Landscape Conservation Movement.*

(4) *Cleator Moor* Collected Poems pp. 14 - 17.

(5) *Whitehaven* Collected Poems pp. 17 - 20.

around the harbour's 'lobster claws'- an evocation of the quay structure. In his topographical writing, as in his other works, the Lake District as recognised by the tourist could not be separated from its industrial coast. In his novel *The Fire of the Lord*, Millom ironworks and slagbanks provide the central setting for the story and where 'The chimneystacks of the ironworks were like the bars of a cage against the sky, and the slagbank heaved its back above the marshes.'[6] The slagbanks, he relates, were themselves tipped on farmland and marshy ground - all factually correct. Indeed this factual recognition of town and its enveloping countryside became the bedrock of the action in the novel.

Whitehaven harbour with the former mine vent, the Candlestick Chimney, in the foreground.

Norman notes, as was typical of his generation, that livelihoods in every town depended on the local industry which, in turn

> was dependent on the locally available raw materials- on the rocks, on the soil, on the sea, on the climate: coal and iron-mining towns, steel towns, ports and fisher-ies, textile towns, built, it would seem, not of brick and mortar, but of pig iron, wool, jute, leather, or clay.[7]

Footnotes

(6) *The Fire of the Lord* p. 50.

(7) *Provincial Pleasures* p. 186.

Such was the nature of England which we have, arguably for economic reasons now lost. This underlined his view that the 'world still needs industry, and - if England is not to become one lubberly suburb, like a great, fat, neutered cat - it will still need its industrial towns.'[8] Thus England is a green and black and pleasant land and wildness in nature and civilisation are equally part of the amalgam.

These trenchant views of Norman stem from a childhood living in the narrow strip of land between Black Combe and the blast furnaces, each towering above and dominating every-day life in Millom. For most of his formative years his friends and neighbours, either directly or indirectly, owed their existence in Millom to the iron furnaces or iron mines. This community, set between the fells and the estuary, did not present a picture of devastation in the landscape but one of support and potential fulfillment and of hope for the future of that community. At the end of his poem *On the Dismantling of Millom Ironworks* and in *Old Railway Sidings, Millom* Norman portrays a community no longer in being. Their loss of employment from their traditional occupations had removed their support in life. The sintered ore as much as the bloody cranesbill were integral parts of that landscape and the people of the town were part of a continuum with their neighbours in the agricultural communities. [9]

Along with the mines Norman had a soft-spot for quarries and their working appendages. Although there is now little trace of the Broad Oak Quarries he knew, his description proves interesting:

> From the quarries at Broad Oak, near Waberthwaite, there is an over head railway, with buckets that sail across the marshes of the lower Esk to Eskmeals, and add - to my mind - another attraction to the view. These aerial railways, and other elemental industrial structures like pitheaps, girders and pylons, seem to fit quite happily into the fells. Perhaps it is because against a landscape that is older than temporal, whereas in an urban landscape, man-made and proportioned to man, they would be hideous and unmannerly.[10]

Footnotes

(8) *Provincial Pleasures* p. 185.

(9) For a full description of how Norman saw the place where he lived see the opening part of his fifth broadcast talk *Enjoying It All* p. 13.

(10) *Cumberland and Westmorland* p. 29.

Millom Ironworks, courtesy of Millom Visitor Centre.

This view would raise more eyebrows of more than a few modern landscape conservationists and his view of the more modern wind turbine construction, especially round the Duddon, may have been perceived as quite controversial in some quarters. However, the point here is not about the merit or otherwise of Norman's opinion but his argument about the human time-depth relationship with landscape. Norman saw the scale of the fells as huge against the puny construction and quarrying works of people.

In particular Norman welcomed slate production from the fells.'Lucky is the townsman who sleeps with a bit of Honister Pass over his head.' (11) he said, putting his faith into green slate roofing. He added

> [l]arge quarries like those at Kirkby and Honister and those in the Coniston-Tilberthwaite-Langdale fells sign themselves boldly across the landscape. Many think they harm it and have protested. It is true

Footnotes

(11) *Cumberland and Westmorland* p. 23.

> that they sometimes add a certain harshness to the scene, breaking up the tones of grass and bracken and heather, but I cannot feel that this is greatly to be deplored. For the quarries are true to the very nature of the rock. They introduce nothing alien […].[12]

Those were the days when the quarries employed many more people than now and what he would make to more modern technological extraction methods with even greater amounts of waste being tipped on the fells must remain conjectural. Again we see how his ability to connect local geology to the lives of the people who lived there.

Only later does he begin to unbend those firmly-held views when he acknowledged, one suspects with great reluctance, that extractive industries are not sustainable when he says mining 'exhausts' and

> A mine is always moribund, bleeding to death at the height of its vigour, so that it is the derelict mine rather than the working mine which becomes permanent in the landscape.[13]

Later he noted the West Cumberland colliery coast contains 'scenery more completely ravaged by industry than any other in Cumberland, but also more dramatic.' He described the scene which today, because of reclamation schemes, we would have to search hard to find any real traces. He concluded the disfigurement is of 'almost Miltonic horror.' [14]

If geology was Norman's first and foremost consideration, then the exploitation of geological resources is almost as vital in understanding his approach to nature. Indeed Norman saw the continuation, to exhaustion, of the mineral bounty of the earth as the way forward for Cumberland's economy but by then, in the 1960s, already showing signs of stagnation and decline. [15]

During his teenage years Norman lived through the slump of the 1920s and 1930s a time the productivity of the Hodbarrow mine declined and the general reduction in demand for iron began to affect employment in Millom. The effect that reductions in wages had on the quality of people's lives was clearly

Footnotes

(12) *Cumberland and Westmorland* p. 27.

(13) *Cumberland and Westmorland* pp. 220 - 221.

(14) *Portrait of the Lakes* p. 171.

(15) *Cumberland and Westmorland* p. 254.

evident in a relatively small community. However, at least Norman reflected also on the positive side of the unemployed practicing their cricket rather than hanging around on the streets in his autobiographical *Wednesday Early Closing*. [16] As the extractive industries made fewer demands on nature so nature began to show itself as it crept back as if in an intrinsic wave of de-industrialisation. [17] In *The Bloody Cranesbill* Norman described the

> Quarries choked and flooded, and all the lovely resistance
> Of blackberry, blackthorn, heather and willow grubbed up and flattened.[18]

It was his boyhood years amongst the industry, the working and unemployed that first instilled the humanity of his poetry and prose. Later it was his enforced sojourn in a New Forest sanatorium that first brought nature into contact with Norman. For Norman, this contrast between the plight of people and the fecundity of nature cemented his outlook of the human condition being an integral part of nature. Human ecology was an ecology as much as that of the local flora and fauna, they were simply parts of the great whole.

Norman included both industrial sites and post-industrial landscapes as central to his understanding of nature. The view that people and their activities were part of life encompassed by nature. The following quotation exemplifies Norman's philosophy that the earth encompasses the natural and the human landscapes:

> I have often thought that the National Trust ought to preserve some typical examples of the landscape created and shaped by industry and then deserted: abandoned ironworks and slag-banks, old clay pits, old quarries, old lead workings, decayed ports, and wharves, brick-fields, gravel-pits, broken-down factories and warehouses, derelict collieries, and worked out iron-ore mines. ...they give a glimpse beyond the scale of history; they set man in a greater perspective of biology and geology, of the pre-historic and the post-historic processes of nature. Here, in the flashes among the slag-banks, or the rubble-heaps of the collieries, we can see nature fighting back, re-colonising the former enemy-occupied territory. It is not a ruin but a renaissance.[19]

Footnotes

(16) *Wednesday Early Closing* pp. 127 - 128.

(17) *Wednesday Early Closing* p. 136.

(18) *Collected Poems* pp. 361-2.

(19) *Provincial Pleasures* p. 107.

Limestone quarry at Hodbarrow, 1980.

Philip Gardner summed this up well when he notes Norman's work reverberates with this theme, one that demonstrates, 'the correct relationship between man and earth out of which he extracts a living.'[20]

Norman found beauty in Millom's iron ore industries, structures and workings that was neither an eyesore nor a polluter of the air he breathed

> [i]n many ways iron-mining is very like agriculture - a root crop, deeply dug, the harvest of which is stored like huge clamps of turnips or mangold wurzels. But it is a crop that exhausts. After the first gathering the land lies fallow for ever.[21]

Perhaps for the first time Norman recognised his advocacy of resource extraction was not sustainable but took comfort that, if the exhausted site is left alone then wild nature would creep back and reclaim the land for its own. He didn't have the foresight or knowledge to guess that modern economics and taste would demand reclamation for further economic use, thereby preventing

Footnotes

(20) *Norman Nicholson* by Philip Gardner, p. 45.

(21) *Provincial Pleasures* pp. 107 - 108.

nature from finding a new habitat. At the time of the closure of the Hodbarrow mines he notes, 'by the time this book is published [the site] will have begun to form a new landscape which I cannot yet clearly imagine.'[22] However, at Hodbarrow, the RSPB have ensured, through managing this site primarily as a place for birds and other wildlife, that Norman's hoped for legacy has to a large extent been achieved.

Hodbarrow's lake in 2013. Note the collapsed inner barrier.

During the years of operation of the Millom blast furnaces Norman notes 'The ironworks stand with their swords guarding an Eden to which, in fact, no one wants to return.' He adds

> A quadruple line of railway, running from the furnace to the mines, keeps out cars as a cattle grid keeps out cattle. Industry, indeed, protects the shore more thoroughly than the National Trust could ever have done.[23]

Norman saw the works as a physical barrier, to all but those on foot, as an access to his beloved shoreline around Hodbarrow Point on the seaward side of the estuary. Given that few people in Millom had cars in those days,it appears an odd, even elitist, opinion for Norman to hold. When considered alongside his views that tourism is a bigger threat to landscape than industry [24] he appeared to be holding views similar to those Wordworth expressed, that access to such secret and precious spaces are for those who have 'an eye to perceive

Footnotes

(22) *Greater Lakeland* p. 129.

(23) *Provincial Pleasures* pp. 146 - 147.

(24) See for example *Greater Lakeland or Cumberland and Westmorland.*

and a heart to enjoy'.[25] In some ways the reference to the National Trust appears contradictory to the earlier paragraph above. Norman appeared never to have fully understood the competences, capabilities or the limitations of a conservation organisation yet, as detailed below, he was a member of at least two such bodies.

Yet despite his love for the extractive industries two matters appear as contradictions. The first, especially in his native Millom, is that Norman could never resist giving the streets natural metaphors, 'The tide flows through the streets as through a delta, through gulley and creek and backwater, along the main canals [...]'[26] This is a fine example of the people and places being in synchrony with their more natural surroundings. Even the town hall clock, its four faces illuminated, is analogous to the Moschatel flower spike, a plant whose other common name is Town Hall Clock. He wrote 'The green-four-face of the clock, like a huge illuminated flower-head of the wild moschatel, blooms into the rain.' [27]

The second was Norman's support for the use of extracted minerals was not, following the second World War, without question as there was one mineral whose use to which he took exception - uranium. Whilst it was not found in commercial quantities in any local rock it was still a geological product and its use in nuclear power caused Norman to have an equal and opposite reaction to his support for the local extractive industries. He notes, 'I am not one who thinks that the splitting of the atom is likely to be a boon to mankind, but Sellafield ... has played a great part in the west coast revival.' [28] After listing the benefits of the plant to West Cumbria, written in the days before the more controversial processing plants were opened on the adjoining site, Norman sardonically noted that a leak from the plutonium piles had caused much locally produced milk to be poured away. He worried that there may be an even greater cost in the human future. The post-Chernobyl effect on Cumbria and the Sellafield scandals may not have helped to change Norman's view on this matter. His objections appear to be based, if only partially, on the fact that the raw materials were not Cumbrian in origin.Therefore, the concept of the atomic plant was alien to his belief that industries should be entirely relevant to their geological setting.

Footnotes

(25) *Guide to the Lakes*: William Wordsworth p. 92.

(26) *Provincial Pleasures* p. 12.

(27) *Provincial Pleasures* p. 14.

(28) *Portrait of the Lakes* p. 176.

Sellafield, a picture taken in 1993.

The other, perhaps main, reason for Norman's objection to nuclear power was its potential to be used for harmful purposes. Having lived through the time of the use of nuclear weapons at Hiroshima and Nagasaki in 1945 and, like many in the subsequent eras, he feared the potential of a nuclear holocaust. Even before the October 1957 nuclear fire at Sellafield (then the site was called Windscale), and in the days after the first use of nuclear weapons, we find Norman fearing a potential atomic holocaust. He sets *Prophecy to the Wind* in a post-apocalyptic nuclear and post-industrial world where the few survivors have mostly returned to a subsistence agriculture. The world is seen as being reversed a millennia and the Icelandic Norse have returned to take stewardship of the Lakeland fells and dales where they dominate the native population, survivors of the next and, this time, nuclear World War. So the landscape around Hodbarrow has become the scene of a new agrarian society trying to live more in harmony with nature. Here Norman portrayed a society less complex than the one he lived in, one with a fear of technology and a recognition that its resources are finite. The suggestion being such an approach to managing resources would provide a blueprint for the continued existence of society.(29)

We find these concerns reappearing later through his focusing on Britain's enriched uranium processing plant at Windscale (now Sellafield). The site had gone through a litany of name changes in an attempt to create a more acceptable public image. His poem *Windscale* expresses his attitude towards the site

> The toadstool towers infest the shore;
> Stink-horns that propagate and spore
> Wherever the wind blows.(30)

Footnotes

(29) *Prophecy to the Wind.*

(30) *Windscale* Collected Poems p. 282.

He also describes the country's first nuclear power station, Calder Hall at Sellafield, as a structure which 'darkens the landscape like a threat' and 'a grotesque hazard for the sliced drives' on the adjacent golf-course. (31)

Whilst the Windscale poem was inspired by the notorious fire in the site's piles that produced plutonium (a material for nuclear weapons as well as, later, nuclear fuel) in October 1957, Norman perceived a threat to the existence of life as a whole from the misuse of nuclear power. In a contemporary poem, *The Elm Decline*, is also useful for helping us to understand how Norman saw changes that the misuse of nuclear energy could effect in the landscape:

Dynamited runnels
channel a poisoned rain,
and the fractured ledges
are scoured and emer'd
by the wind-to-wind rubbings
of nuclear dust.'(32)

The result of all this would be an earth, he believed, where the land was devoid of all life and for which

no human eye remains to see
a landscape man
helped nature to make.(33)

Footnotes

(31) *Greater Lakeland* pp. 159-160.
(32) *The Elm Decline* Collected Poems pp. 283 - 295.
(33) *The Elm Decline* Collected Poems pp. 283 - 295.

Chapter 3: The Rural Landscape
"High on the Corried Slopes " [1]

Norman's awareness of the agricultural community and rural economy around Millom started in his schooldays. Being a keen scholar Norman absorbed some of his local knowledge from the school, as also from his fellow pupils. Some of his classmates were farmer's sons (in those days the school had separate boys and girls classes). The milk deliveries also brought him into contact with the farm that supplied to his father's house. His father sold clothes to the farming community and the young Norman came to know better the rural hinterland of the town. The inter-dependence of the urban and rural economies provided, as would be typical in a small town, natural everyday occurrences of social interchange. The rural landscapes which entangle the agricultural life of his home area were opened up through his ascents of local fells and local rural rambles and cycle rides. People working the land and animals in the landscape became as much a part of his immediate world as the miners and iron workers who were the bedrock of Millom's economy. To Norman the rural and the industrial were equivalents because they involved real people in their adaptation to their respective habitats. Yet Norman did not know sheep and cattle farming as well as he understood the more extractive industries. But his interest, not least in the traditional upland sheep farming traditions was great and provided him with a time-depth relationship with the rural landscape. Norman found farming a link with his Norse ancestry as these settlers were amongst the line of Lakeland sheep farmers and who occupied farms still strongly recognisable today.

It was when he began to explore the hinterland of Millom that Norman better discovered sheep farming. Then it was more typical small mixed farming enterprises with crops and animals the norm rather than the more specialised farms we find around the area today. It was the typical farm we find in *Haytiming* [2] when the wet-cut hay is making competing demands on farm time with the aftermath of the lambing season, or when the ewes need to be clipped for their wool production - all then a vital and integral part of the farm economy for each smallholding.

Norman's creation of Tyson, a statesman farmer, was used as an example of a typical upland farmer in The Bow in the Clouds[3], and this poem shows a fur-

Footnotes

(1) *Cloud on Black Combe* Collected Poems pp. 323 - 324.

(2) *Haytiming* Collected Poems p. 344.

ther reference to Norman's appreciation of the agricultural industry. Norman continued to he developed an interest in this way of life with his understanding of the sheep farming traditions of hefting, where lambs and gimmers [unmated female sheep] being taken onto the fells to their home patch by the ewes. This world of the upland sheep farmer is a poetic subject for Norman but equally forms a significant focus in his topographical writings. (4)

Sheep farming at Wallabarrow.

In The Bow in the Clouds (5) we can understand the way Norman saw the natural linkages - the estuary, the shore, the pitsteads, agriculture and the wildlife - all with a common spirituality. There is the risk of trivialising the other meanings within this long poem. We can read of the portrayal of the changing light on the landscape and people's lives, the changing tides and seasons of nature which provide a canvas on which human activity not only depends materially but from which we, as an integral part, are able to find our spiritual needs.

Footnotes

(3) *The Bow in the Clouds* Collected Poems p. 103-111.

(4) *The Land Under the Ice* Collected Poems pp. 116-121.

Whilst Norman had, as we saw in the previous chapter, made some criticisms of the excesses of the extractive industries, he was also aware that farming had to be sustainable in the interest of future generations. It was the heavy demands placed on resource using industry in World War Two that perhaps makes this point. Norman was aware that resource depletion could not continue beyond a very short time span, if that. What he would have made of more recent issues of over-grazing on the fells and the excessive use of artificial fertilizers and pesticides must remain conjectural when considered against his background of arguing for the sustainable use of the land:

You treated the earth, then like a mother;
You gave worship in your work and took the fruits with thanksgiving.
But now your guts are tight with greed:
You tear the crops like hair from a living skin;
You drive the earth like a slave; you wring
The last drop of blood from the land till the soil is dried into dust.
The hills which were your altars have become your middens;
The becks which were your temples have become your sewers.[(6)]

Shortly after in this verse play The Old Man of the Mountains, a fine old ash tree is to be felled 'it's time it came down and got turned into money'.[(7)] Later in the same play we find the criticism re-made as his biblically based character Elijah suggests:

They gaze with miser's eyes
On the God-given landscape; they ravage the harvests,
Shovelling the gold grain into bellies and money-bags:
They wrench the trees from the living pores of the earth,
That gropes its roots deep in the brain of the rock,
Sags and droops like a bramble, because the blood
Is dried in the veins of the men of the dale.

and then, by contrast, we find a call for sustainability:

Humbly to accept the gift and grace of the seasons,
To tend the earth like a mother not a slave. [(8)]

Footnotes

(5) *The Bow in the Clouds* Collected Poems pp. 103 -111.

(6) *The Old Man of the Mountains* pp. 11-12.

(7) *The Old Man of the Mountains* p. 13.

(8) *The Old Man of the Mountains* pp. 48-49.

This play was written in the war years (though not published until 1946) when not only were the ravages of essential increases in food production laying waste to the land but also when there was a major national campaign to designate national parks as an essential part of the peace dividend. It was not fashionable to be a conservationist at this time but Norman was laying down arguments and principles of which the related nature and landscape conservation movements would have readily accepted.

Norman treats farming as synonymous with the fine landscapes he knew, like others he regarded agriculture as the creator and the maintainer of those landscapes. The Lake District is a cultural landscape which displays a strong link between current land use and a recognisable historical dimension that can be traced back over several thousand years. This significance, a major factor in the potential bid for the area to be recognised, technically inscribed, as a World Heritage Site. This linkage would have appeared a natural argument to Norman as one of his most popular poems testifies:

> The wall walks the fell-
> Grey millipede on slow
> Stone hooves;...
>
> They build a wall slowly,
> A day a week;
> Built it to stand,
> But not to stand still.
> They built a wall to walk.[9]

Despite this recognition, Norman was capable of confusing wilderness with wildness, an error still prevalent amongst current conservationists. Today wilderness is largely reserved to describe areas with little or virtually no readily apparent human impacts. Whereas wildness, as well as being a human state of mind, is more aptly used to describe a tract of land where there is a feeling that nature is richer than found in most humanised landscapes. Until 1965 the importance of Common Land, of which the Lakeland fells contains over thirty per cent of England's registered common land, was not really widely appreciated. This shared grazing on land owned by someone else is fundamental to the understanding of Lakeland fell farming as it is to appreciating the landscape of the open fells. So, there is a tension to be found when Norman writes

Footnotes

(9) *Wall* Collected Poems p. 321-322.

A fell wall, Long Green, Troutbeck.

that he and thousands of other people had a love of the fells and yet they hold a sense of quietness and openness 'and we take a vast joy in lifting up our eyes and our hearts ...unto the hills and among them and upon them.' He added

> [y]et why the hills? Why should they have this fascination for so many? I think it's because the hills, in the bare, unpopulated, uncultivated parts of the earth's surface, you can see our physical environment reduced to its simplest terms: rock, water and air.[10]

Yet within this broadcast series of talks, printed as *Enjoying it All*, we are forced to have our transient existence made clear, that we can see the earth is viewed as relatively everlasting. Robert Macfarlane, a well respected academic and current writer on literature and the outdoors, explains this transience

> it is a physical as well as a cerebral horror, for to acknowledge that the hard rock of a mountain is vulnerable to the attrition of time is of necessity to reflect on the appalling transience of the human body.[11]

Norman's view of the farming landscape with its annual cycles of birth and death, of growth and decay, set against the slower cycles of geological change, are fundamental to understanding his rurally focused writings.

Norman was entranced specifically by the Herdwick breed of sheep as have been many Lakeland writers. For Norman it was also the lives of the Herdwick farmers and the long tradition of the management of this breed which he focused on in his topographical writings about the Lake District. Norman writes that the Herdwick had dispossessed the red deer as claiming 'the freedom of the fells.' He adds

> These sheep are not wild, nor are they able to get on without the aid of men, but they have adapted themselves completely to their habitat, and they play an essential part in the life of the dales. They owe their existence not to sentiment but to practical value.[12]

Norman was intrigued about the hefting of sheep - where each ewe maintained

Footnotes

(10) *Enjoying It All* p. 5.

(11) *Mountains of the Mind* p. 43.

(12) *Cumberland and Westmorland* pp. 79-83.

its own place in the flock on the open fell, a tradition each mother teaches its lamb. The clipping of symbols in the ears of the sheep to show their ownership (called lug marks) and the, now almost extinct, method of counting the flock in what Norman called 'Celtic' scoring numerals (and others call Norse scoring numerals) fascinated him. Depending on the Lakeland dale, where variations are found the one to five count might be heard as yan, tan or tyan, tethera, methera, pimp. (13) Again the cultural and the natural were so intertwined that any attempts at separation would be regarded as folly.

Footnotes

(13) For more information on the fell farming traditions including the counting system the reader is directed to *Life and Tradition in the Lake District* by William Rollinson (1974, London: Dent)

Herdwick ram.

Chapter 4: Landscape Change
"The birds soon found sites that the Council couldn't. " [1]

Norman, as we found in chapter 1, was acutely aware of change over geological epochs as well as the relatively faster rate of attrition caused by geomorphological processes. In one book, *Cumberland and Westmorland*, he recognised that the landscape was not only changing but perhaps at a rate of attrition greater than we would think from our everyday perceptions. Not only are we reminded of the agents of change through frost, sun, wind, rain and rivers but 'the estuaries are silting up; ...the dunes are blown into shape; ...the tarns are slowly filling up' provided but three examples.[2] He even suggested that if the estuaries are silting up then people might accelerate the process by reclaiming land - exactly what had happened around the fringes of the Duddon and Morecambe Bay - long before Norman wrote this piece. Of the dynamism of the estuaries he was not obviously fully versed. Whilst, in chapters 2 and 3, in examining his approach to human interactions on an industrial and agricultural scale, the acceptance of change was clearly apparent. Norman adopted a similar approach to rural landscapes.

It was not just recent human landscape change, for Norman fully understood that the landscape was the product of over four millennia, change effected since the arrival of people as far back as the Stone-Age. Whether this was brought about through subsistence or unsustainable exploitation rarely matters, what is more important to Norman is the time-depth appreciation of human interactions with landscape he brings to his work. Near Millom are a series of stone circles at Kirkstantion, Lacra and, arguably, one of the Lake District's most dramatic sites at Swinside. In his poem written on a wet day at Swinside called *The Megaliths* he recognised that these deliberately placed stones, perhaps from as far back as 4,500 years b.p were the works of people who had started to inhabit the post-Ice Age landscape. This land of forests and fellside juniper existed prior to clearance by those early inhabitants for a more settled agriculture life. Vegetational change by people on a large-scale results in a change of habitat and catalyses a change to the nature of that area. However, change undertaken by people can be far more rapid and dramatic than natural succession. [3]

Footnotes

(1) *Bond Street* Collected Poems pp. 304 - 305.

(2) *Cumberland and Westmorland* p. 48 - 49.

(3) *The Megaliths* Collected Poems p. 150.

The later clearance of the primeval, native woodlands appears in Normans work in his depiction of a conversation between a raven and a beck in his verse play *The Old Man of the Mountains*. Here Norman described the aftermath of the woodlands on the fellsides and recognised these as areas we now see covered in bracken, a fern he thus regards as a 'stranger'.(4) Today, we recognise that if we want to create new native woodlands in the fells then the bracken-covered slopes have the potentially better soils.

This decline in woodland cover of the early peopled landscapes is best explained in Norman's poem, *The Elm Decline*, which describes the bare post-glacial landscape that was colonised initially by primitive plants and then the flowering plants and trees. He then describes how the pollen record (in cored peat samples) shows there was a dramatic decline in the number of elm trees that covered the landscape at around 3,000 BC. This, he explains, was caused by

> Stone axes,
> chipped clean from the crag-face,
> ripped the hide off the fells.
> Spade and plough
> scriated the bared flesh,
> skewered down the bone.(5)

Such an approach to the ecological history of the landscape was perhaps first started in Wordsworth's *Guide to the Lakes* in 1810 and was continued in later topographical writings, including Norman's own, by many later Lake District writers. It can be considered as a natural reaffirmation of the whole view of human ecology that we trace back to the Romantic writers.

There is a strange paradox for, if we regret the loss of much of the native landscape of the pre-human era, then should we still value the much-loved open character of the Lake District fells today? If we talk about re-wooding the

Footnotes

(4) *The Old Man of the Mountains* p. 11. Bracken was once regarded as a woodland fern but the extensive tracts on the Lakeland fells are, more often than not, a typical part of the landscape. The fact is it is a result of long-term and possibly unsustainable agricultural and woodland practices. [NB: in the Lake District and the Peak District (and elsewhere) bracken was harvested 'sustainably' by local farmers for animal bedding and in the glass-making/chemical industry. The bracken-covered hillsides of today are as a result of changes in farming and industrial practices in the twentieth century; prior to that the bracken was kept under control in small patches/fields harvested on rotation.]

(5) *The Elm Decline* Collected Poems pp. 283 - 285.

Swinside stone circle.

uplands today then we run the charge of badly affecting the important cultural depth of the sheep farming tradition of the area. With such a change we would also alter the widely regarded openness of the fells, both in terms of extensive views and of a sense of personal freedom. Yet the change that shaped today's open landscape was the result of unsustainable exploitation of the fells which the Romantics would find in antipathy to the conservation ethics that these writers gave rise to. However, we still call this, in a particular English fashion, natural beauty. [(6)] There was a further contradiction, which I shall quickly pass over, Norman admired the open fell landscapes but found stretches of moorland dreary. Given their common origin and contribution to the upland landscape, there are some people, especially those from the Pennine mill towns, who would find this admission extraordinary.

Norman used the poem *The Elm Decline* to explain an unsustainable or a misuse of economic development, especially nuclear power, and how it could lead to the extermination of nature and of the human race. It was the latter thought which concerned him most of all. Yet, he did not fully understand how the traditional local industries might also be unsustainable. He appeared to believe that once people had finished changing the landscape then nature would reclaim the sites and all would be well. Somehow there was no human responsibility to nature during this devastating process because communities benefited from such processes. Nor was there an allowance for, what we now call brownfield sites, being reused for employment purposes once the first use had declined. We have to accept that, by modern day standards, Norman's values could appear contradictory to us.

Footnotes

(6) For an explanation of the origin of this usage see my *Thirlmere and the Birth of the Landscape Conservation Movement.*

That said, the vital message of this much undervalued poem, *The Elm Decline*, is to assert that humans are part of nature and not a different kingdom to the flora and fauna. Around the same time, Norman wrote a poem about the estuary mosses (largely what we refer to as the salt-marshes), *September on the Mosses*, where he cautions that once we begin along the path of unsustainable change then, when the tide has turned, we cannot hold back its flood over the mosses. [(7)]

Norman's description of the history of Oldborough (the fictional Millom) recognised that change and development are part of a constantly evolving landscape and community. The physical growth of the size of a community is tied, obviously, to changes in population as well as to changes in the size of new building plots. He saw such changes as a neutral observer, neither enthusiastically welcoming nor condemnatory. It is to Norman part of a natural evolutionary process. In Millom the more 'native' inhabitants were greatly outnumbered by the influx of Cornish and Welsh miners and ironworkers who migrated here to meet the demands of the developing iron industries - the mines and the furnaces. These workers came to where the geology provided the raw materials. With them came their traditions, not least the influx of worship in the Protestant chapels and their associated social life, one that formed a contrast to the deeply embedded Church of England and, to a lesser extent, the Roman Catholic traditions. Much of this influx occurred prior to Norman's birth but it had an effect on his upbringing, not least that his step-mother was a Methodist where his father and his birth family belonged, at least in allegiance if not practice, to the Church of England.

During Norman's early life, the ironworks and mines were major employers in the town. They dominated the lives of the people, the landscape setting and the development of the town. In short they gave Millom its character, one in which Norman was readily immersed. Yet he could still dispassionately recognise and observe as an integral part of the whole life of the town. However, during his life came times of economic hardship through a recession, the Second World War, a run-down of resources and then stagnation and abandonment of its' whole purpose of being a community. For many people, this produced industrial dereliction as well as economic decline and social hard-

Footnotes

(7) *September on the Mosses* Collected Poems pp. 288-289. The estuary mosses are now regarded as the lowland raised bogs that surround the Duddon and the Morecambe Bay estuaries (and are mostly nature reserves) and the estuary side salt-marshes or saltings which are vulnerable to tidal inundation.

ship. But Norman saw such changes as endless treasure chests for his writing. The people

> as the early town flourished and decayed around them, did not change face, kept themselves to themselves, held bones together with a slapping of cement.', a place where one character lived, 'in one of t the few undemolished houses of Marsh Edge Street.[8]

Change in the industrial landscape was occurring as far back as in the 1950s when the 'old Ore Pier [from where iron ore from Hodbarrow mines was shipped] was abandoned long ago.' [9] The railway lines were taken up during Norman's lifetime but the fossilized indentations of the sleepers 'are still marked in wild thyme, and the track makes a thoroughfare through the ragwort and sea holly.' [10] The changing physical remains of past industry are read as an integral part of a newly naturalised landscape and where

> [i]n the histories of the twenty-second and twenty-third century this spot will surely look very much the same as all other ruins in the hills round about - the Roman Camps, the Bronze Age barrows, the flint factories and the stone circles.[11]

The temporal world of archaeology was still present as new sites were evolving to become future artefacts in the landscape. Thus de-industrialisation and abandonment created new habitats for nature, and the recognition that brownfield sites can be precious wildlife resources is a matter in which some wildlife experts are now only starting to appreciate. Yet, Norman had foreseen, from the beginning, the value of such sites becoming available to nature.

Another example of his vivid description of an area of post-industrial change is found just away from the mines,

> Further inland, about a hundred yards from the shore, the railways begin to spool out of their tangle of parallels, and there are cinders mixed into the sand, and knuckles of ore rolled under brambles like lost cricket balls. Wagons stand abandoned beside

Footnotes

(8) *Provincial Pleasures* pp. 134 - 135.

(9) *Provincial Pleasures* p. 43.

(10) *Provincial Pleasures* p. 143.

(11) *Provincial Pleasures* p. 144.

> broken-down buffers or toppled over at sand-chocked points, and the stonechat perch upon them as if the red of their breasts were intended by nature for camouflage among rust.[12]

In another case, he is the reporter, observing the change from the pumped hollow where the Hodbarrow haematite mines once stood. On the mine's closure, the pumps were switched off and the water flooded back into an area which was originally occupied by the sea. There is a personal family connection, through his uncle, with mining at Hodbarrow and there is a huge change to the landscape, sometimes locally referred to as the creation of the Lake District's most recent lake. Yet, there is no value judgement from Norman just a simple reporting of nature, represented by coot and moorhen, as it reclaims the huge, former industrial site. [13]

Whilst much of Norman's output is often without value judgement, as can be seen when he describes changes in the landscape, this is not always the case. One major change is best illustrated when he described the closure and dismantling of Millom iron works. The poem, *The Dismantling of Millom Ironworks*, provides a vivid description of the physical demoli-tion of the huge industrial site which had dominated the landscape. This was the place he had

The remains of Millom's old pier by the Duddon estuary.

Footnotes

(12) *Provincial Pleasures* p. 147.

(13) *Hodbarrow Flooded* Collected Poems p. 279.

known all his life and its closure represented the loss of the dignity of employment -tinged with deep regret. [14] Here we have a swift and dramatic change to a landscape with which he had a lifetime's acquaintance. Norman shows the common trait of humankind's inability to accommodate this kind of large-scale and rapid change to something that is familiar. For many people this is the kind of change that kindles the NIMBY [not in my back yard] spirit in us. The NIMBY accusation is often used in an attempt to belittle the modern day conservationist. Whilst there is a relationship between the two concepts there are significant differences. The key point here is how we react to changes that are huge and irreversible, to places with which we already have a deep affinity. We normally think of, change occurring gradually throughout the human time-span but a more rapid change tends to unsettle many people. Almost a reverse to this is the speed of geological change which we seldom notice as it occurs over, relative to our lives, the eons of time. Norman represents such change 'the rocks seem to be about the most permanent things in the world around us.'[15] Whilst the poem, *The Dismantling of Millom Ironworks*, referred to

Hodbarrow miner. Picture courtesy of Millom Visitor Centre.

Footnotes

[14] *On the Dismantling of Millom Ironworks* Collected Poems pp. 359 - 360.

[15] *Enjoying It All* p. 5.

was first published in 1981, it has echoes of Norman's almost identical views, written in his novel *The Green Shore*, in the years following the great depression of the 1930s.

Norman was a paid-up member of at least two local conservation organisations, the *Friends of the Lake District* (FLD) and, he was a founder member of what is now known as, the *Cumbria Wildlife Trust* (CWT). He made it clear that whilst he had a general empathy for the aims and objectives of these charities, landscape and nature conservation bodies respectively, he did not agree with them in every respect. Both organisations appreciated, and still do, constructively critical members, of which Norman was one. In some cases his recorded views, for example as we have seen earlier on industrial development in rural areas, were diametrically opposed to the specific views of the organisations, particularly of the FLD. However, such views never caused him to waver in his fundamental support for the need to conserve and enhance the special natural and landscape qualities of the greater Lake District. Indeed, some of Norman's views would set him back into the picturesque tradition - rather than his inherited Romanticism. Afforestation was a significant case in point. Yet Norman appreciated that special qualities are necessary for human inspiration, for re-creation, and for spiritual values. He joined these conservation bodies because he shared their concerns about what was special and, despite some of Norman's unwarranted criticisms, saw the need for people to influence the rate, scale, nature and direction of change, if the supporters of such bodies were not to lose all that was dear to them. In that, he was a true Romantic and never accepted the divorce of people from nature.

However, Norman did display a lack of understanding in the way such organisations worked. He accepted the way of thinking, too often aimed at the conservation movement, that conservationists are out to preserve the landscape in aspic. He notes,

> I feel their attitude is based on the desire to preserve the Lake District. Now that seems deplorable. Lord preserve us from the preservers. I am hag-ridden with the prospect of the dales becoming a museum.' he adds, 'The only way to prevent this is for the dales to continue as a living economic unit,[…][(16)]

Footnotes

(16) *Cumberland and Westmorland* p. 61.

Had he troubled to talk more to the organisations that he criticised, and was a member of, then he would have realised they were singing from the same hymn sheet! Preserve the *genius loci* yes, but manage the rate, scale, nature and direction of change to ensure it is a sustainable living landscape with a historic cultural dimension: this would be the shared battle cry. Indeed later in the same work Norman agrees, with respect to the FLD's work, '[n]o one wants to see the dales covered with unnecessary dams, girders and pylons, and the Friends of the Lake District are right to be wary,..' and added '[l]et us watch out instead for umbrella tea-gardens, Tudor cafes, red-tiled hotels, unnecessary motor-roads over the passes, speedboats on the lakes and motor-cycle tracks on the hills.'[(17)] Yet, there are some people who think today that CWT and FLD have little to do with the needs of humanity, yet as registered charities this must be their first consideration.

A few years later, in 1949, Norman admitted, in print, to his FLD membership and said he no longer needed to complain about the activities of the Friends. Not that he would admit to his views having changed, but he believed with the greater prosperity in the post-war generations, the Lakes had become more connected with the remainder of England economically and socially. Therefore it was society that had changed! What was needed was the FLD and the national park authority to fight against commercial exploitation.[(18)] That said, Norman did appear to have a problem in splitting those economic activities which he thought were beneficial and those he found exploitative and unwelcome in a way that would have drawn universal approval.

In one poem, *On a Proposed Site for Council Houses, Holborn Hill Ward, Millom Rural District*, Norman almost undertakes the weighing of the balance between development and protecting the open space of the site. In this case he believed development could be a beneficial change to the landscape as it provided houses for people to occupy whilst considering the flora and archaeology of the proposed development site. [(19)] These are just the kind of issues that affect the FLD and CWT to this day.

Footnotes

(17) *Cumberland and Westmorland* p. 209.

(18) *Portrait of the Lakes* p. 181.

(19) *On a Proposed Site for Council Houses, Holborn Hill Ward, Millom Rural District* Collected Poems p. 185.

One of the issues where Norman's views again varied from the conservation bodies was quarrying. But again, there is the caveat that slate quarrying in the 1940s and 1950s was on a much smaller-scale and more labour-intensive activity than current higher technological slate quarrying, with its greater volume of waste rock. Norman notes,

> The quarries which provide the stone are no ill features of the landscape. From a distance they look like scars, but only the pock-marks on an old man's face. Giving character to it. Individually, however, they are of great charm. I am thinking now not of the large commercial quarries ... but the small fellside pits, each to give a farmer stone to build a byre or make a road.[20]

Thirlmere reservoir in the 1990's

Even now few, if any, conservation bodies would disagree with him but the cost-benefit analysis of such operations means there are precious few of this type of operation remaining in the Lake District. Again, it shows the danger of looking for examples of Norman's views, rather than his underlying philosophy, in the range of his writings.

Footnotes

[20] *Cumberland and Westmorland* p. 17.

Even with quarries we find that Norman's assumption, which only too often proved unfounded, that such sites will eventually be abandoned to nature and where change would naturally occur in a way that '[e]verywhere the angular, almost cubist, man-made facade of the rock is being smudged back into the unobtrusive smoothness of nature.' [21]

Norman notes, in his topographical Cumberland and Westmorland, that Wordsworth had opposed the planting of larch and quoted him as saying that the planting of this tree species produced 'great injury to the appearance of the county.' Norman accepted that this alien species could be naturalised and found 'The larch has certainly settled down, and there is not a lovelier green among the fells than the April green of the larch.' [22] As he notes, in the context of differing views on the aesthetic merits of new conifer plantations in the Lake District,

> [i]t is wrong, I think, to regard the District as an album of views, the sole purpose of which is to please the beholder. The District, indeed, is a living part of the countryside, having its own function in the life and economy of the nation. Its beauty is only a by-product.[23]

Yet, later, he comments that some introduced conifers at Haweswater acted as 'a police force of conifers forbidding you to go near the water.'[24] Norman certainly had strong views, ones which he articulated with supporting reasons and we should avoid the morass of trying to read into his individual (and time-dated) views as to what he saw as beautiful. Instead, a concentration on an analysis of what was Norman's underlying philosophy of nature and its relationship to humanity is necessary.

For Norman, it was paramount that people should regain the understanding that they are fully part of the landscapes and habitats. To conserve and preserve species and views is inspirational, provided people realise that they are not detached but integral to such actions.

Footnotes

(21) *Greater Lakeland* p. 68.
(22) *Cumberland and Westmorland* p. 55.
(23) *Cumberland and Westmorland* p. 59.
(24) *Greater Lakeland* p. 85.

Slate quarrying, Bursting Stone Quarry, 1963.

The Hodbarrow Miner, Millom, 2012.

Great Horsetail

Chapter 5: The Lower Plants
"The Spore box of the moss." (1)

It may appear strange to have a chapter devoted to the so-called lower plants - the non-flowering plants of the Cumberland countryside - mosses, liverworts, algae and ferns, along with the inaccurately labelled part of the plant kingdom, the fungi. To many people such organisms hardly exist, part from the colourful fungi and edible mushrooms often, but wrongly classified together. These plants are less apparent to the casual observer than the more colourful flowers, they can be minuscule and some are very rare but, equally they can, like bracken, appear in attractive mass Autumnal colours on the fell-sides.

That Norman took a keen interest in these taxa despite them having a low-profile public persona, is a measure of how good Norman's botanical skills were and the depth of his floristic interest. Norman's writings about plants exemplify what Melvyn Bragg describes as Norman's approach to seeing his local flora 'he has kept his eyes firmly in front of his feet and discovered an evident relish for botany,[…]' he was, he said, 'a bard with the eye of a botanist.'(2) Whilst this is seen with lower plants it is equally apparent in the way he responded to flowering plants (see next chapter).

Norman saw the geology, and the lichens which encrust the rock surface. Amongst the slag heaps he saw the early colonisers, plants which not only came before the flowering plants in the story of evolution but which also tend to be the first to colonise bare ground.

The earliest plants, still found today, to emerge this earthly life-giving group are the algae. Many of these plants are tiny but they also comprise our seaweeds. Norman reflected on seaweeds' relationship within a shoreline habitat (on rocks and in a rock pool) for animals: 'bladderwrack, baked dry as crust on top, but, below, a simmering moisture of crabs and whelks and mussel-shells.'(3)

Footnotes

(1) *Above Ullswater Collected Poems* p. 143.
(2) *Between Comets - for Norman Nicholson at 70* pp. 57 - 58.
(3) *Provincial Pleasures* p. 149.

The horsetails are well-known (and often hated), by many gardeners, being invasive plants that are virtually impossible to eradicate. They are plants which find and exploit bare places of earth often in places where soil quality is poor. Norman described field horsetail bursting forth in spring on disturbed ground. He reflected on how such a plant can be successful when its life-cycle can fall within a narrow window of opportunity such as where Norman describes horsetails as 'Anxious to get on with the job of seeding.' (4) Such fecundity of spores enables the plant to find its niche, to grow, reproduce and then to decay annually to leave a residue which assists the formation of future soils (5). He also found time for the horsetails in *Provincial Pleasures*. He notes, 'at the front of the slagbank the horsetails prick up their brown periscopes to see if it is time for the fronds to come out.'; an accurate description of the germinating field horsetail (6). Later in the season, in May, he recognised the much less common great horsetail and, its preferred habitat is, as with some other special flowering plants, 'desiccated bony places.'(7)

Toadstool is a common name for a number of fungi which, scientifically speaking, are not plants - but perhaps this is the right place to include them. In Norman's day, this non-plant distinction was rarely made and students were taught they belonged to the plant kingdom. However, in regard to these organisms Norman's observational abilities exceeded his knowledge as he looks at how some fungi can be problematic in our lives: appearing as or causing diseases in nature. He does not appear to have written how, without the work of some fungi, the plant and animal kingdoms would not exist - and therefore neither would we. One problem of these plants was the subject of a poem written around 1953, *On Suspected Dry Rot in the Roof of a Parish Church.* (8) His comparison between structures at Sellafield and the stinkhorn fungi is found at the end of Chapter 2.

In the relatively tiny backyards of their back-to-back houses of Millom some householders would grow plants in pots whilst other plants could grow on their walls, air pollution allowing. In many cases these plants were taken as roots from their natural habitats, local to the area, as Norman tells us in *Pro-*

Footnotes

(4) *Horsetails Collected Poems* p. 49.

(5) *Horsetails Collected Poems* p. 49.

(6) *Provincial Pleasures* p. 105.

(7) *Provincial Pleasures* p. 110. However, great horsetail is often also found in damper locations in Cumbria.

(8) In Collected Poems pp. 409-410.

vincial Pleasures. One of the commonly selected groups of plants for growing were the ferns, which were amongst Norman's own personal favourites. Norman was always proud to show his visitors the specimen of royal fern kept in his backyard. This plant was gathered by his father from local mosses and continued by Norman. [9] This plant was the subject of a poem in which he described it by its generic and scientific name, *Osmunda regalis*.[10] We also find, in what he describes as Mrs. Grice's terraced house backyard - but most likely based on his own home with additional observations from those of his neighbours - the description,

> [i]n old barrels and up-ended chimney pots are great
> oil-gushes of ferns - Lady Fern, gathered among the mines;
> Royal Fern, gathered from places that few know on the
> Dunner mosses; and the Maidenhair Spleenwort and
> Hart's Tongues that have come there by themselves.[11]

The royal fern, quite uncommon in Cumbria, can still be found on the Duddon Mosses, which is now a protected site, designated as a Site of Special Scientific Interest and a National Nature Reserve.

He also found a rarer, for Cumbria, coastal fern 'The sea-spleenwort grows in exactly the same crack as that where it was recorded sixty years ago.' [12] There are now over two-hundred plants of sea spleenwort to be found along this stretch of shore.

Norman, as we shall see in the next two chapters, dedicated single poems to an individual plant or animal species. The nearest we get with ferns is the observation of the maiden-hair spleenwort

> On quarry walls the spleenwort spreads
> Its green zipfasteners and black threads,

Footnotes

(9) Norman's father had original planted a virginia creeper in some soil he imported. The yard gained windows boxes with daffodils and geraniums but other plants naturally colonised the yard. These included dog's mercury, herb Robert, lesser periwinkle, lady's mantle, primrose and dog rose.

(10) *A Garden Enclosed* Collected Poems p. 233-234.

(11) *Provincial Pleasures* p. 135.

(12) *Provincial Pleasures* p. 149.

Royal Fern.

Sea spleenwort at Hodbarrow.

> And pinches tight its unfurled purses
> In every crevice with the cresses, [...] [13]

Two relatively uncommon and difficult to find ferns, so much so any botanist delights in seeing them are adder's tongue and moonwort. It is a tribute to Norman's observational skills as a botanist that such plants became regarded by him as amongst his list of the local specialities that he delighted in finding. The list also includes the sea spleenwort and the great horsetail both mentioned above. [14]

His fascination with ferns and non-flowering plants extends to his topographical writing,

> Of mosses, lichens, horsetails, grasses and fungi I won't try to speak, but the mountains of Cumberland and Westmorland are, of course, a fine place for ferns. Many of the rarer species grow there - Tunbridge filmy fern, Wilson's filmy fern, oblong Woodsia .., holly fern, oak fern, green spleenwort. The bracken I have already spoken of, and parsley fern is also very common, but is much more confined to rocks and hills. It is a lovely little fern, with its barren fronds very like parsley leaves that it is named after, and its fruiting fronds quite distinct, with narrowed segments, standing more upright. When the latter are covered in spores, they are a rich chocolate brown, beside the barren fronds, which remain a light green throughout the summer.[15]

He goes on to describe hard, lady, male, royal, adder's tongue, and parsley ferns, and all demonstrate how good his personal observation was.

Footnotes

[13] *Rockferns* Collected Poems p. 47.
[14] *Wednesday Early Closing* p. 135.
[15] *Cumberland and Westmorland* p. 74.

Adder's tongue fern.

Chapter 6: Flowering Plants
"Pimpernel and speedwell sparkle in the soil" [1]

Norman's botanical interest was wider than plants which were special or rare in any sense. Even the common varieties, which in urban areas most people don't even give a second glance, were to Norman an intrinsic part of the local character. Whilst at the ruined castle in Egremont he noted mouse-eared hawkweed, groundsel and ragwort on the poorer soils adjacent to the ruined castle. [2] To Norman they formed an integral part of this historic site and, given the insignificance of such plants to most people, it reflects his holistic acceptance that the works of people and those of nature are irreversibly intertwined. We find in the poem, *Egremont,* a fascination with these seasonal and transitory plants. Annuals with interesting seeds were recognised late in autumn, when there are no obvious flowers by which most people would identify the plant. Thus the plants survive for another opportunity to seed and grow in the coming year, just as the human relationship with nature is not seasonal but constant. In *Provincial Pleasures* we have a monthly account of life in and around Millom. Each month provides a glimpse of locally found wildflowers - many commonplace but some only found by those with questioning eyes.

Norman tells us that

> [t]o a botanist, a flower is of great interest largely in proportion to its rarity.' and then adds, 'I want, ..., not to give a list of rare or even common flowers, but to try to say what flowers are typical of one or two types of country in the district.[3]

This he successfully achieves in the next pages of Provincial Pleasures as he ranges from the fells, the mountain pastures, the coast, the coastal marshes, the lowlands and the mining sites. The flowers are all special to the finder, even if common species, but people are taught not to divorce them from the whole landscape. What makes that landscape special is the assemblage of plants with their geology, their topography, their land use and how they relate to our lives. We cannot truly separate any part of nature from the landscape or from our humanity. We are an intrinsic part of nature.

Footnotes

(1) *The Anatomy of Desire* Collected Poems pp. 159 - 161.

(2) *Egremont* Collected Poems pp. 14-15.

(3) *Cumberland and Westmorland* p. 62. See also the subsequent pages (pp. 62 - 74).

Norman's botany, as noted in the last chapter, included a knowledge of botanical Latin names - their generic and specific binomial. Winter heliotrope, more strictly a garden 'escapee' and an invasive pest for some nature conservation sites, is not only accorded its full binomial but Norman gives an account of its habitat where he found the plant around Millom, the form of the plant and, its less frequently observed floristic details. [(4)] The same source provides us with evidence of Norman's approach to botanical accuracy - 'and the once-blue sea-holly is merely a pin-cushion of empty grey calyces.'[(5)] Norman also provides observations as to how mountain pansies, like other flowers, close up their inflorescence in dull, damp weather conditions 'shut up and fade'.[(6)]

In his homage to Wordsworth and the River Duddon, Norman placed riverside plants into their habitat and their place in the landscape:

> From becks that flow out of black upland trans
> Or ooze through golden saxifrage and the roots of rowans.

Downstream we find other species:

> Through wet woods and wood-soil and woodland flowers,
> Tutsun, the St. John's-wort with a single yellow bead,
> Marsh marigold, creeping jenny and daffodils;[(7)]

Many of these flowers can still be found along the river Duddon today especially the native wild daffodil.

To Norman the habitat of a plant was synonymous with the landscape, there was no artificial distinction, as many conservationists had inherited from 1949. [(8)] We can read his descriptions of places plants grow as much as botanists would use the word habitat and others would use landscape. The Burnet rose is found on the Cumbrian seashore:

Footnotes

(4) *Provincial Pleasures* pp. 30-31. .

(5) *Provincial Pleasures* p. 153.

(6) *Cockley Moor, Dockray, Penrith* Collected Poems p. 27.

(7) *To the River Duddon* Collected Poems p. 25.

(8) The National Parks and Access to the Countryside Act of 1949 was probably the benchmark in making this false distinction.

At the sea's kerb, at the wide
Turn of the dune
The burnet rose
Grows in its green
Ravel of leaves, like seaweed,
White as bare flesh
When the bright June sun
Flows in on the flush of the tide.[9]

There are a number of Norman's poems dedicated to a single flowering plant species, an accolade he also bestows on a few animals (see next chapter). Examples of these include the bramble or blackberry. In this poem the form of the berry is a metaphor for our connection with nature. In this particular case, reflecting how Norman demonstrates how people can find spiritual refreshment in nature:

And grant to us the sense to feel
The large condensed within the small;
Wash clear our eyes that we may see
The sky within the blackberry.[10]

Wild daffodil by the River Duddon.

Footnotes

(9) *Song* Collected Poems p. 32

(10) *The Blackberry* Collected Poems p. 48.

But Norman's eye was not simply fixed on a single species but often on a single flower of a single plant, and at a very close distance. One high-summer flower of the wetter areas of ground (wet flushes) in the Lake District, where it can occur, very locally, in large numbers, is the grass of Parnassus. This plant occurs in two poems in the 1948 volume *Rock Face*. In one poem it is accorded two lines:

> Grass of Parnassus, with wax Spanish combs
> Which the green scum of duckweed smirches,[...][11]

Then we find a poem dedicated entirely to this flower with a description of the landscape and community in which it is found followed by a very detailed observation of a single flower:

> Brittle and metallic, white and veined
> Like the iris of an eye -
> Perfect as a birth beneath the catastrophic sky.[12]

Grass of Parnassus.

Footnotes

(11) *The Land Under the Ice* Collected Poems pp. 116 - 121.

(12) *Grass of Parnassus* Collected Poems p. 147.

Finding this flower, in wet, misty weather conditions in the lee of a wind affected how Norman saw beauty and wonder in the most unpromising of circumstances. The delight and contrast of a sudden, unexpected discovery brings value to what has been seen in a way that reawakens our delight in the appearance of even a common species.

Norman's description of the life cycle of an oak tree from the awakening of an acorn, through to the flowering tree, maturity, senescence and then to fire-wood takes us through a process longer than the human life-span. This palimpsest of all the stages to be seen around us is placed within a single narrative as if it were happening in a continuous process before our very eyes. It takes us through the setting of the tree and its ecology, for the oak is our most important tree for the numerous other plant and animal species to which it gives life. A large and vital part yet, such a small part of nature, is an oak tree and a human being. (13)

Arguably Norman's most effective poem describes a single plant found, in Norman's youth as today, on the outer barrier of the Hodbarrow Hollow near the iron lighthouse. Usually, this is one of the most unpredictable flowering orchids; it sometimes turns up on disturbed ground, often along the coast where it has not previously been recorded. With the bee orchid we are taken through Norman's usual range of ecological and cultural affinities of a plant, in this case through the context of its site at Hodbarrow, through the immediate habitat and then down on to our knees to see the individual florescence.

> Decoy queens,
> Honeyed and furred,
> Linger and cling
> To each lolling lobe;
> Nervous green-veined,
> lilac sepals
> Prick at the twitch
> Of a pollinating wing.(14)

The earth can be seen from the minute to the wide vista and if we adjust our focus, when we stop and look, we can see not only a great deal more of the world but also the human place in the whole scheme of things.

Footnotes

(13) *The Oak Tree* Collected Poems pp. 227-228.

(14) *Bee Orchid at Hodbarrow* Collected Poems pp. 276 -278.

Bee orchid.

Later in life, although obvious throughout his output, Norman stated his love of wild plants and especially those native to his shore and fell hinterland. Whilst he had time for garden plants it was a strong love of what nature provides in his landscape that appealed to him far more than cultivated flowers. This was especially the case when such flowers are produced for commercial purposes. Playing on the much misused title "Weeds" - Norman is saying that no wild plant is insignificant even if its name is unknown to us and even if it is growing where a gardener might not want it to grow. One example is the very small flowered and insignificant appearance of fat hen, a plant equally as vital to Norman as the rarer, more showy bee orchid.[15] His message appeared to be that bought, cultivated flowers make us blind to the natural way a plant grows and without seeing the context of that flower we are blind to the natural processes that we are part of, and which enrich our lives.

Another flower which meant a great deal to Norman is the bloody cranesbill. This was due to him finding it originally as a youngster during a local fam-

Footnotes

(15) *Weeds* Collected Poems pp. 341 -342.

ily amble and then later in life returning to the site near Hodbarrow to find the plant for himself. This is a dramatically coloured purply-red flower found along the Cumbria coast and Norman gives the species his usual full inspection - from the context to the petal:

Was Sunday's flower, the Bloody Cranesbill, red as the ore
It grew from, fragile as Venetian glass, pencilled with metal thread
Haematite-purple veins. The frail cups lay so gently
On their small glazed saucer-bracts that a whisper would have tipped
them over
Like emptying tea leaves out.[16]

Again, we find a poetic description of a fragile looking assemblage of petals set in an industrial and post-industrial landscape where other plants are also reclaiming the closed haematite mines and spoil heaps for their own. Yet this time, we have the personal family dimension representing the relationship of people within the natural world. He allows the same treatment of the ploughman's spikenard, a plant Norman claims to have discovered as a first for Cumberland whilst exploring the Hodbarrow area.[17] Finding the plant for the first time in the Hodbarrow area, although he had seen it around Arnside previously, reflected his ability to be a very able observer of the finer details of the components of his landscape.

Footnotes

[16] *Bee Orchid at Hodbarrow* Collected Poems p. 361 -362.

[17] *Portrait of the Lakes* p. 42.

Bloody cranesbill.

Chapter 7: Animals
"Wings in a Flummox of Feathers" [1]

Whilst Norman could be described as a botanist (a label he refuted) the same could not be said about the level of his knowledge of the animal world. When a TB patient, his interest in all living things was enhanced through his reading and he did become a keen observer of fauna especially of birds. As with geology and botany Norman's interest showed itself initially in some of his early work. The early war poem *Corregidor* features eagle, jellyfish, squid, octopus and sting-ray, all within the poem's 21 lines. Here the eagle is the scavenger feasting on the animate jetsam thrown up by the attrition of tides on a rocky headland. The casualties of war are sacrificed so that the raptorial beast can thrive, even with clipped wings.[2] His limitations around animal ecological knowledge are shown, for example, in his frustrating inability to distinguish the footprints of different mammals.[3] Partly made up for with a sheer list of species, one poem mentions around 20 different kinds of animals, and includes the names of rarer species like twite, a bird which might be found around the coast near Millom especially in winter.

His most extensive writing about animals can be found in his topographical works especially in a chapter devoted to 'Creatures Great and Small'in Cumberland and Westmorland. This section comprises a collection of myth (the death of the last wolf in England), a deviation from wildlife to the ways of farming the Herdwick sheep, of sheepdogs, but mostly about birds. The final section of this chapter, on the coastal gulleries, is now very dated, as they have mostly disappeared, but it offers us the prospect of seeing how change, largely through human agencies, resulted in a significant change to the composition of the local fauna (and flora) within the last few decades.[4]

As a keen wanderer along the littoral, Norman frequently reflected on the wonders of sea-shore life and here his admiration of the natural world is often at its height. The barnacle is found on local rocky shores where it is 'scattered over the rocks like little cement-mixers, ...preparing to open their shutters

Footnotes

(1) *A Match for the Devil* p. 39.
(2) *Corregidor* Collected Poems p. 3.
(3) *Provincial Pleasures* p. 133.
(4) *Cumberland and Westmorland* pp. 77 - 95.

to the tide.'[(5)] Here we have Norman using, unusually, a metaphor with an inanimate comparison to explain the nature of the wildlife rather than his expected use of wildlife to explain a physical feature or human activity in the landscape. An early example of the natural metaphor is found in the war poem, *The Evacuees* , when Norman ponders what life will be like for World War II evacuee children if they have a prolonged stay in Millom:

> Will they rest,
> Will they be contented, these
> Fledglings of a cuckoo's egg reared in a stranger's nest?[(6)]

The descriptions of various animal species and their ecological and human habitats are common themes throughout Norman's writings. The metaphor of the evacuee children is mirrored for the young eels which he observed in the drains used for pumping water away from the hollow occupied by the Hodbarrow Mines and described in his poem *The Elvers*. The young eels would have migrated back from the Sargasso Sea to Hodbarrow from where their parents had left to breed. Whilst the poem takes license with how we understand the ways by which young eels ascend a flow of water coming out from the mines, we are left with a sense of great mystery as to why the eels undertake such an arduous journey. [(7)]

England's only poisonous snake, the adder, lives on some of the coastal and moorland habitats known to Norman. Like all similar reptiles it has a forked tongue for detecting the scent of its potential prey. The metaphor for indicating one course of action and then taking another is 'to speak with a forked tongue' or 'talked in a snake's voice'. It was the language Norman used to describe the girl he met at Sunday School and appeared to Norman to encourage him to make advances but then spurned his proffered love [(8)].

It is birds Norman observes and understands mostly in the local faunal kingdom. As a TB patient Norman learned to identify a number of birds both visually and from their song as they carried out their day-to-day activities in

Footnotes

(5) *Provincial Pleasures* pp. 149 - 150.

(6) *The Evacuees* Collected Poems pp. 53-54. Norman was party to the knowledge of a nest, found containing a cuckoo's egg, and which was being guarded by workers at the Hodbarrow iron-ore mines, until it fledged.

(7) *The Elvers* Collected Poems p. 275.

(8) *Love Was There in Eden* Collected Poems pp. 6 - 7.

Adder, sometimes called a viper.

and around his New Forest sanatorium chalet. Yet he may be modest in this admission of his ornithological knowledge for earlier in life he noted that thrushes rather than blackbirds appeared to be more common in Millom.[9] He also observed his grandmother's caged linnet:

> [t]he bird itself was a sadly drab, dull-brown creature, cooped up in a space not much bigger than a biscuit tin. Unlike its species in the wild, it never put on the cocky spring plumage, the russets and terracottas, but spent the whole year disguised as a female.' [10]

Are these the observations of a young ornithologist in the making or is it the reflections of knowledge gained later in life about a remembered facet of his early life?

In winter bird migrants from Scandinavia including the redwing arrive in Cumbria: 'gregarious thrushes with surprised yellow eyebrows and under-

Footnotes

(9) *Wednesday Early Closing.*

(10) *Wednesday Early Closing* pp. 53 - 54.

wings that look bloody as from a wound.' (11) A behavioural description that some other casual ornithologists might find revealing. The redwing also features in a poem where it, and his appreciation of Grieg's music, like the Norsemen who may, as he claimed in his poem *Cornthwaite*, have been his ancestors, came from Scandinavia 'Crossing the sea with the migrant redwing.' (12) Whilst talking to Norman about setting some of his poems in an audio-visual presentation, in the early 1980s, he expressed the view that Grieg's chamber music was one of the most appropriate sources against which to set his poetry. Norman also shared his knowledge of how the tides in the spring affect the arrivals and departures and the resting of the migrant birds in the Duddon estuary. His description of an albino robin further reflects his sharp focus on detail whilst still retaining the bird's behaviour. (13) The description is used to demonstrate the difficulty of how a disadvantaged person might struggle to fit in with a small, provincial community.

The Lakeland fells have, for many eons, been a relative stronghold of the raven, a bird almost wholly associated with the uplands. In a poem, *Raven*, Norman describes the mountain habitat where he had seen the bird.Here we learn a little about the raven's biology but a great deal about it's symbolic values as they would have been as part of the everyday folklore of the tenth- and eleventh-century Norse settlers to the same area.(14) In the prologue of his verse play The Old Man of the Mountains it is the raven that acts as the narrator, the voice of God. The description of the relative isolation of the bird's February nest high in the fells captures brilliantly the habitat of this most characteristic of upland birds. The raven is now more common, even in the relative lowlands of Cumbria, than it was in the early 1940s. At that time the bird was persecuted by farmers and gamekeepers, as it was regarded as a threat to new born lambs. Norman, with a simple phrase, raises the bird from perceived vermin to be equal with people in nature 'I am not always as black as you see me now...' , the raven's would-be persecutors are belittled as the dales folk who 'crawl like ticks in an old sheep's wool.' These are the people who ignored the voice of 'created nature' and are those who 'Yet many times you do not listen.' (15) Attitudes have changed a great deal since those trigger-happy days when it

Footnotes

(11) *Provincial Pleasures* p. 29.

(12) *For the Grieg Centenary* Collected Poems p. 36.

(13) *Provincial Pleasures* p. 32 - 33.

(14) *The Raven* Collected Poems p. 59 - 60.

(15) *The Old Man of the Mountains* p. 9 - 10.

was quite a common occurrence for birds with hooked beaks or the crow family to be shot if found on rural estates.

One bird, which is rarely seen in England and then most often on migration, still nests in very small numbers on the cliffs of St. Bees North Head, as was the case in Norman's time. This bird, a largely Arctic species, the black guillemot is accorded a poem of that title. The poem describes the setting of the cliffs with the superb views across the Solway, the flora on the cliffs and the lines of nesting birds hugging the cliff face as they incubate their eggs. However, the few black guillemot are mixed in with a much larger number of common guillemot but it is these commoner birds which Norman apparently described. Both birds are similar in shape with black backs and white bellies but the description of dozen on dozen facing the cliff whilst sitting on their egg can only refer to the common guillemot. The distinctive white wing patch of the black guillemot is not mentioned. Yet Norman appears to have been aware of this difference, as he makes clear in an almost contemporary writing, when he recognised the razorbill and both species of guillemots at St. Bees North Head in his topographical stroll around this part of the coast and notes 'the black guillemot, of which this is the only breeding place in England.' whilst the common guillemot are 'huddled close as carrier pigeons in a crate.'[16]

Despite this error the mood of the poem's picture reflects the bird galleries on the north-west coast's most stupendous cliffs which are bedecked with wild flowers (and our less common fern Sea Spleenwort) and set against the wide sea. Here there are views to the Isle of Man and across the Solway to the Galloway area of Scotland. Inland you can see to the highest Lake District fells and the site offers a genuine feel for the special qualities of this unique part of the Cumbrian coast. Norman also provides an understanding of the strong parental sense the birds have in ensuring the success of their annual shore visit to lay eggs and nurture their off-spring. The black guillemot, a single species, albeit misnamed, has its life set within a superb ecological, geological and dramatic landscape. [17]

Footnotes

(16) *Greater Lakeland* p. 162.

(17) *The Black Guillemot* Collected Poems p. 271.

Another bird, the chough, which used to nest on the same cliff faces is no longer present. However, its current nearest breeding grounds, on the Isle of Man and Anglesey, can be seen from Cumbria. The Isle of Man is, opposite St. Bees Head, at its nearest point to England, being some 40 kilometres to the west. The chough, was described by Norman as the Cornish chough. Cornwall was, at the time he visited the St. Bees area, perhaps its last English breeding area, and appeared to have been no longer breeding on the Cumbrian cliffs. Current work on ensuring the close-cropped fields provide an ideal feeding source for this cliff-nesting bird gives rise to the hope that it will once again return to its former haunt. It is, as Norman described '[o]f all the rarities, it is the red-billed Celtic crow that I would most like to see back again at St. Bees.'(18) Another rare bird Norman recognised at St. Bees was the peregrine falcon. This is another species that has become more widespread thanks to conservation efforts after the banning of agricultural poisons that were thinning the birds' egg-shells and so impeding breeding success. The success of the increase of this species would have delighted Norman immensely.

Footnotes

(18) *Greater Lakeland* p. 163.

Black guillemot.

St Bees North Head

Chapter 8: Natural Metaphors
"Watching the changing arguments of the clouds" (1)

In previous chapters it is clear the use of a naturalistic metaphor was an integral part of Norman's writing style - be it poetry, fiction, drama or topographical writing. Several such metaphors have already been highlighted as have, but rarely used, metaphors where Norman has asked us to compare human artefacts resembling nature. The nuclear piles of Sellafield being "stinkhorns' (fungi) is perhaps the most extreme natural example. There is also the context that much of Norman's output was also allegorical with the natural world serving to provide a moral meaning. A meaning which was sometimes religious, but more often, spiritual or pertaining to the human relationship with nature.

In his homage to William Wordsworth Norman, as did the Grasmere poet himself, uses the course of the River Duddon as a symbol for the life of a human. The river starts life in mossy springs high on the fells, it has a tumultuous youth before slowing down in old age and then, finally, meeting its maker, the sea,within the estuary. The sea evaporates, clouds form and the prevailing winds return the water to replenish the mosses: 'eternity flows in the mountain beck.' (2)

The Duddon poem was one of Norman's earlier writings but the theme continues throughout his writing. A rocky fragment derived from the erosion of the fells becomes patterned pebbles on the sea shore and they are 'grained like a bird's-egg.'(3) Of St. Bees sandstone, this Permian rock of the sea cliffs, we find 'The stone is grained,/ Smooth as walnut...'.(4) We are invited to see 'ferrets of fire' / Glide through the age-old / Forest glades.' when we look into a coal fire.(5) The metaphor is used explain nature and how it so integral to human activities.

We find botany becoming an intricate part of a floral analogy for the iron-works:

Footnotes

(1) *A Match for the Devil* p.53.
(2) *To the River Duddon* Collected Poems pp. 24 - 26.
(3) *Silecroft Shore* Collected Poems pp. 170 - 175.
(4) *Seven Rocks* Collected Poems pp. 242 -251.
(5) *Put on More Coal* Collected Poems pp. 391 - 392.

From the tundra of despondency
A carboniferous humus flames into fruit.
Hundred-million-year-long latent spores
Germinate green in a burning spring; ferns
Unfurl in hearth and furnace - crackling bracken
And spleenworts of fire. On winter slagscapes
Smoky-branched larches drop their clinker cones,
Lockets and nuggets of sun. the world's one flower
Shale calyx raising a combustible corolla
To the sky's one seed.[(6)]

The subtlety is in using natural examples that can be found within sight of the furnaces. The maidenhair spleenworts inhabit the local walls, the sea spleenwort the coastal rocks. The named parts of the flower reflect the earlier poem *Bee Orchid at Hodbarrow*. A further device he used was of applying flower colours to Christian values:

For red is faith, the colour of pimpernel.
For orange is hope, the colour of marigold.
For yellow is charity, the colour of lady's bedstraw.
For green is temperance, the colour of marram grass.
For blue is prudence, the colour of chicory.
For indigo is justice, the colour of bladderwrack.
For violet is fortitude, the colour of deadly nightshade.[(7)]

Again, all the examples are of flowers Norman knew from his home area, all potentially found within sight of the the various local churches and chapels that played some role in his life. Notwithstanding Norman saying he had neglected botany the great majority of his examples of metaphors taken from the natural world come from plants. However, geological and faunal example are never far away. There are times when he emphases his underlying knowledge of the natural world when he quotes the binomial generic and specific names as for the plant pearlwort:

Footnotes

[(6)] *Affirming Blasphemy* Collected Poems pp. 411 - 413.
[(7)] *The Bow in the Clouds* Collected Poems pp. 103 - 111.

> Inconspicuous as a money -spider:
> *Sagina procumbens*,
> The herb of the pearl.[8]

Examples can be found in his prose writing in particular:

> [...] the small reedy lakes of Grasmere (the grass lake) and Rydal (the valley of the Rye) are cupped like a thistle-head in a calyx of green and spiky fells.[9]

And:

> The first Ironworks buzzer wakes me at five-thirty - a long dinosaur moo, followed by two short snorts, [10]

If there is a theme running through the metaphors it is that Norman was so deeply imbued with a sense of the natural world, the world of rocks, plants, animals and natural processes that he was fundamentally a nature writer. Throughout his life his love of the outdoors and all its natural wonders influenced his range of writings. Nature was more fundamental to him than any of his other interests and proved a more prolonged foundation for his life than his religious beliefs. His understanding of nature was the one that the earlier Romantic writers would have recognised in that it placed humanity as an integral part of the greater meaning of nature. People are part of nature but not dominantly so, and the message to humanity is to take our place amongst the plants and animals on Mother Earth.

Footnotes

[8] *Pearlwort* Collected Poems pp. 425 - 426.

[9] *Greater Lakeland* p. 60.

[10] *Provincial Pleasures* p. 33.

Millom locals, 1980.

Chapter 9: People in Nature
"I become part of a landscape" [(1)]

Whilst much of Norman's output links the nature, landscape and habitat in both urban and rural places, and without making the current artificial separations between such concepts, there is always the link between nature and humanity. The dimension of people, their lives, their needs are essential to understanding his work and, whilst they had the utmost importance in his thoughts, they were never separated from nature nor seen to be dominant over nature. This outlook is more akin to his earlier Methodist chapel teachings than to his later Church of England allegiance. He notes, '[i]n Odborough [i.e. Millom] a man may seem a long way from the centre of things, but he is closer to the heart of things.' He added 'He sees the soil, the hills, all about him.'[(2)] The lives of the people of Millom were lived integral to their immediate surroundings and, as time went by, to their wider hinterland. The celebration of the provincial is because of the town's human roots being intermingled with the foundation rocks and their overlying sedimentary deposits.

Norman wrote a short series of poems during and after a visit to Norway in the mid 1970s. They were followed shortly after by a poem about his middle name, Cornthwaite, one with Old Norse roots.[(3)] The juxtaposition of these works reflects the time-depth continuity he saw in the human ecology of the landscape. His middle name Cornthwaite is linked to settlers who arrived in Cumberland. The area around Millom is now called Copeland, a name itself derived from Old Norse, in this case loosely translated as 'bought land'. This millennia-old settlement of his home area is reflected in the number of names of places in the sub-regional landscape which are derived from the times of the Norse settlers. Descriptive words such as tarn, beck, fell, and thwaite, are found in almost every Cumbrian dale and were often expanded through the use of personal names or descriptive titles. Some of the flora and fauna that was familiar to the Norse settlers, still existed in Norman's day (as much does now). The sheep farming traditions in the uplands owes something of its time-depth to the cultural influence of the Norse settlers and, whilst evolution-

Footnotes

(1) *Thomas Gray in Patterdale* Collected Poems p. 141.

(2) *Provincial Pleasures* page 190.

(3) *Cornthwaite* Collected Poems p. 354. The Norway poems includes the often cited Sea to the West and this is found in the same volume pp. 338 - 339.

ary change has occurred, the *genius loci* of the essential spirit of the landscape away from the industrial and urban fabric of Millom, can still be felt. This human-nature relationship was fundamental to Norman's epistemological beliefs and thus to his writing.

The smallness of humanity in the natural world can be seen in Norman's poem, *Footnote to Genesis II*, where Norman alters the perception of the human perceived dominance over nature to that of an equal status and partnership. We can read this in his comparison of humans with birds, where humans are just another species sharing Mother Earth:

> There is no word for bird in the diction,
> For man himself has improvised their songs and man
> From his lantern eye, clicked at the flick of movement,
> Projects and colours feather and fantail, tawny and tan.

And, later

> In the avian evening, creatures
> That are what man means by bird have their own word for man.[(4)]

A decade earlier he had fundamentally already noted,

> [f]irst, the gradual breaking down and rebuilding of the rocks by the action of water; and second, the dying down of vegetation in autumn and its rebirth in spring. Every form of animal life, including that of human beings, has to fit into those patterns. We are made of just the same elements as the rocks, and the cells of our bodies work in the same ways as organic nature everywhere. We depend on the rock, on the soil, on the seasons, on the seed-time and harvest. We can help to modify the workings of nature to grow things; we can adjust the balance here and there. We can assist nature to grow things; we can discourage nature from growing other

Footnotes

[(4)] *Footnote to Genesis II, 19, 20* Collected Poems p. 231. The Bible text reads: verse**19**: 'Now out of the ground the Lord God had formed every beast of the field and every bird of the heavens and brought them to the man to see what he would call them. And whatever the man called every living creature, that was its name. **20**: The man gave names to all livestock and to the birds of the heavens and to every beast of the field. But for Adam there was not found a helper fit for him.'

> things. But we can't break out of the pattern. If we try to make nature behave in an unnatural way, then, eventually, we will starve ourselves out or blow ourselves to bits.[5]

His central point is that whilst many humans think they control nature whilst many humans believe they control nature they should realise this is illusionary. This is illusory and any human idea of dominance could be the down-fall of our species - a message current and relevant today as ever. People are, as any reading of Norman will demonstrate, an integral part of nature.

Footnotes

[5] *Enjoying It All* p. 15.

Millom 1980.

Chapter 10: Conclusion
"One life is knitted into another" (1)

It is important to recognise from the outset that Norman's religious belief became, for a large part of his life, fundamental to his everyday existence as to his writing. What I have tried to show is that his spiritual belief enhanced by his interest in the great outdoors had a much longer-lasting and more fundamental foundation on his work and his outlook on life. This can be demonstrated through his understanding and commitment to nature, to landscape (be it agricultural, urban, industrial or more natural), and his devotion to people who lived and worked in his physical and spiritual hinterland. This holistic approach to people as a constituent part of the wider living world remains fundamental to an understanding of his work. If we believe that Benjamin Fell (his fictional character in the novel *The Fire of the Lord*) is speaking for Norman then we can understand how paramount nature was to Norman's understanding of life, and that his spiritual beliefs were wider than concentrating on his religious observances would have us understand:

> We build churches and chapels and cathedrals and this and that and the other, and we think we are praising the Lord, but we're only putting a roof between ourselves and the Lord. We ought to get out into the fields, into the highways and hedges and praise the Lord there.(2)

This passage is from his first novel *The Fire of the Lord* that he wrote a few years after he returned to being an active Christian.

Most systems of early religions and spirituality, from pagan to Hinduism and Confucianism as with a number of current belief systems, share a commonality of being underpinned by a reverence for nature. Trees, mountains, springs, for example, were natural features that took on sacred meaning particularly before such occurrences could be scientifically explained. This connection between nature and spirituality underpinned Norman's adult life. Yes, at times, he was an overtly Christian poet but we cannot understand that dimension of his work without more fully appreciating that the spiritual-natural bond was

Footnotes

(1) *Provincial Pleasures* p. 36.

(2) *The Fire of the Lord* pp. 62 - 63.

more long-lasting and deep rooted. Without this appreciation his Christian output lacks intensity and full meaning. As Neil Curry writes '[h]is love of the Lake District and the extent of his knowledge, even his geological knowledge of the area, are inseparable from his awareness of its spiritual quality.'[(3)] Yet Curry rarely identified Norman's due position as a nature poet and writer.

Norman's second novel, *The Green Shore*, showed his holistic approach to his local habitation. Again Odborough is Millom and all the places mentioned in this work, despite the huge scale of de-industrialisation in and around the town, can largely still be located in some form. The community was bound up in the local industry and associated trades and, in large part, to the regimes of church and chapel in the 1940s. The spiritual life of the novel's main characters is founded on a sense of place, on the local geology and natural history. 'The walls were of limestone from the quarry' [(4)] is amongst the many references to the real Millom. Much of Norman's work was based on real landscapes as they worked better than surrogate, imaginary places. Knowing an area intimately gives to inspiration for a writer or for an artist. As Melvyn Bragg notes, 'he has kept his eyes firmly in front of his feet and discovered an evident relish for botany, geology and the rumps and remains from previous cultures - especially the Norse [...]' [(5)]

But in *The Green Shore* it was the rarer or more special species he found in the local landscape (and mostly still can be today) rather than the commoner species, the ubiquitous chaffinch, blackbird and privet hedge, that are notable features in this novel. Three extracts readily illustrate Norman's depth of knowledge of his home acres:

> [t]he cliffs below the tidemark were black with bladderwrack.[(6)]

Seaweeds are largely found on rocky coasts and, whilst bladderwrack is a common species, few areas of the Cumbria coast have rocky foreshores. His local coast at Hodbarrow is such a place.

Footnotes

(3) *Norman Nicholson* by Neil Curry p. 13

(4) *The Green Shore* p. 129.

(5) *Between Comets for Norman Nicholson at 70* p. 58.

(6) *The Green Shore* p. 9.

> Curlews flew over them, gurgling and calling, casting shadows over the sand.[7]

Curlews can found around most Cumbria estuaries in small numbers, as around the Duddon, and are associated with the uplands where they often nest on moorland. Yet the call is so distinctive and evocative. And:

> [n]earer, on the red rubble heaps, horsetails were waving their green whiskers, and wild mignonette grew on waste stone beside the shaft.[8]

Horsetails, at least the field horsetail, may invade gardens but there are other less common types to be found in the area add this to the less-well recognised mignonette and Norman is clearly demonstrating the special character of the Millom area.

This symbiotic relationship between people and the rest of nature can be seen as fundamental to Norman's thoughts when man, he writes,

> depends as he always did on the sun, on the forces of air and water, on the fertility of the soil on the yearly renewal of the green world. For many men, indeed, this fact is obscured by the mechanisation of society. They forget it with their minds; but in their hearts they know it to be true.

He adds:

> [f]or today, as much as ever, man needs to adjust himself to the seasonal rhythm of nature, the growth of grass and tree, and the alternation of sun and wind and rain.[9]

People are seen by Norman as partners in a dynamic and mutually beneficial relationship with nature. He counsels people should recognise their life is a small part and they should not act to unsustainably extract, determine or attempt to rule over the kingdom of life.

Footnotes

(7) *The Green Shore* p. 85.
(8) *The Green Shore* p. 104.
(9) *Provincial Pleasures* p. 68.

There is a danger in trying to separate different themes within Norman's volume of works. Such was his wide compass of local knowledge which set the *genius loci* of Norman's writing his readers are always brought back to the salient and fundamental point of always regarding his work with aholistic recognition of his depth of awareness of the interdependence of the natural and human landscapes. Such a principle mattered to Norman as it informed and underpinned, in a constant and consistent manner, his life and work.

Any reading of Norman's work must give due recognition of the contemporary history, of the decades in which they were written. Yet they can also be read in a contemporary manner. Norman was a modern-day Romantic writer centring his work on a place where people and nature intermingled as they still do to-day. There is no need to approach his work with a solely religious expectation although for some of his works this might be a more appropriate way of approaching their interpretation. The personal spiritual messages arise very much within the self and the more we know about nature, the rocks and the place of his work then the deeper are the meanings within the poems, plays and novels. This fundamentally natural approach is more overt in Norman's topographical writings. The reward from experiencing nature with Norman as a guide to the landscape, the habitats and their nature, the urban settings of people's lives and work is greater if we take a more secular, holistic approach to his work.
There is also Norman's personal approach to exploration to heed. Rarely did he get his feet wet in paddling on the shore apart from early visits there with his grandmother. Norman, whenever physically able, cycled and walked extensively in the hinterland of Millom but never admitted to having an adventurous escapade amongst the fells. Norman did not admit to scrambling or climbing or shimming up trees. Norman did not have sublime foundations for his rural journeys, his approach was to be more of an observer with the most genteel of physical attachment to his subject.

If there is a physical presence that best encapsulates Norman's sense of people, nature and place being parts of the whole, then it must be the fell that dominates the landscape of Millom and so overshadowed the life of Norman - Black Combe. Barely disguised as Black Fell in *Provincial Pleasures* the fell overshadows much of Norman's creative output. Many years ago, whilst preparing an audio-visual talk based on some of his poetry I was searching for a title for the talk, perhaps 'The Man who Lives beneath Black Combe'. Alas brevity suggested the words 'who lives'could be deleted. Norman sipped his malt, a twinkle came into his eyes, and he said 'I'm not yet dead'. The Black

Black Combe.

Combe part was regarded as entirely appropriate. Indeed for Norman the fells were not just a means of escape but a fundamental backdrop to everyday life. This started when he was a young boy being raised amongst the urbanity of the streets of terraced houses with the dominant presence of the iron-works on one side and the fell bearing down on the other. One was seen from the front of his house the other from the back. A clue to this presence of Black Combe is given in his autobiography (*Wednesday Early Closing*) when referring to an influence on his early life, Marmaduke Fawcett, but without an explanatory context. Here we read of this early power of the fell: 'there was something of the strange strength that I was already begin-ning to sense in the mountains' [10]

We find this omnipresence of Black Combe:

> [i]n October, winter begins its siege of the town. The
> horizons are smudged out. Black Fell is no longer a ladder
> to the loft, but a stone rolled against the gateway,
> blocking the road.[11]

Black Combe was a frequent point of literary reference even if not always named. This reached a crescendo in the 1981 volume of poetry *Sea to the West*, which contains three poems with the fell name in the titles. Two of these

Footnotes

(10) *Wednesday Early Closing* p. 85.

(11) *Provincial Pleasures* p. 164.

(12) The three poems are *Cloud on Black Combe*, *The Shadow of Black Combe*, and *Black Combe White* Collected Poems pp. 323 - 329.

poems are particular focussed on the relationships people experience with natural processes such as climate and weather whilst the third links with the fell with the inevitability of human death. Together these three works show how Black Combe shaped the landscape of life in Millom and how its presence was inescapable. Thus we have the welding of rocks, natural, elemental processes, the flora and fauna and the human interaction symbolised by this fell.(12) The poems *Beck*, *Wall*, and *Clouded Hills*, from the same volume, may also have been influenced by the fell.

Black Combe is in many ways unique. The largest block of any Lake District fell in terms of the area of its base and the most isolated fell from the central 'wheel hub' of Lakeland peaks. From the summit is a significant vista looking, at the most distant recognisable places, to Scotland, Ireland, Wales and Staffordshire on those especially clear days. It was a fell that Wordsworth, for the above reasons, also felt unique. In Wordsworth's poem, *View from the top of Black Comb*, we find a more detailed list of the most distant landscape features. In discussing the geology of the fell, rocks called by geologists the Skiddaw Slates, Norman notes 'Black Combe (which is the largest outcrop of this slate in the south of the county) is the sphinx itself.' (13)

As we saw earlier, a parallel to Black Combe was the physical boundary of land for Millom - the coast from Silecroft and then the significant estuary of the River Duddon. This coastal strip presented a rawer edge of nature for Norman. The dynamic interplay of sea and land, erosion and accretion, land gained, land lost, plants established, plants washed away along with the daily tidal regime and the seasonal changes in climate and bird migration held a huge fascination and draw for him. This was also a coast of industry and people. This area received the weather created by Black Combe as the fell made the clouds rise and cast their rain load onto the coastal belt. It was a frontier only in terms of physical access for Norman. Again it was the 1981 volume *Sea to the West* that produced the culmination of Norman's inspiration from this experiential landscape. *Shingle*, *Dunes*, *Tide Out* and *Plankton* give the substance to the title poem of this volume. (14)

Footnotes

(13) *Cumberland and Westmorland* p. 16.

(14) These poems can be found between pp. 324 and 333 in *Collected Poems*. The title poem *Sea to the West* is found on pp. 328 - 329.

On this narrow strip of land and the breadth of the sands we have, in *Sea to the West,* Norman's life and it's setting for his ecological philosophy. The youth who looked to the sun and the tides, to these natural processes to influence him in his maturing years and on to his nearing death as the light disappears below the horizon but with the certain knowledge that nature and life would continue to influence humankind for time immemorial. 'he gave back a voice to the landscape..' remarks William Scammell who edited the volume of tributes from other writers and poets for Norman's seventieth birthday.(15)

Not for Norman is Blaise Pascal's

> mingled wonder and horror at the realization that man is poised teeteringly between two abysses: between the invisible atomic world, with its "infinity of universes, each with a firmament, its firmament, its planets, and its earth", and the invisible cosmos, too big to see, also with its "infinity of universes", stretching unstoppably away in the night sky.(16)

Norman saw the whole picture of the relationship between people and nature at both an elemental and spiritual level and, for him, there is no abyss, because from atom to universe was but a continuum of that which nature and humans are but a living part.

This continuum can be seen in his introduction to the works of William Wordsworth where for nature:

> the Way is not confined to the countryside but applies to the whole of the created world, to the whole world of matter. A sacrament, or a defilement, can be made equally of a sea-shell or even a handbrush as of Saddleback or Helvellyn.(17)

Footnotes

(15) *Between Comets for Norman Nicholson at 70.* p. 10.

(16) Taken from Robert Macfarlane's *Mountains of the Mind* page 45 A writer whose current interest are based on geology and nature in a similar vein as Norman.

(17) *William Wordsworth -An introduction and selection* pp. xxv -xxvi. The last two names are Lakeland Peaks, the first more often referred to as Blencathra.

As Neil Curry so correctly points out:

> [i]t was as early as 1951 that Norman Nicholson wrote his critical biography of William Cowper and so perhaps did not realize how doubly appropriate was its final sentence: In his precarious pilgrimage he looked at a few feet of grass about him, at the creatures he saw, or the fireside he knew, with a love wide enough to include all Nature and all his fellow-men, and with the sharp tenderness of a long Good-bye.[18]

There is, within many parts of the current conservation movement, a down-casting of hope for the future. The stresses caused by unrestrained economic growth and physical development are often key to this concern. Locally the pressure of tourism rather than discovery of the great outdoors (a point Norman made in his topographical writings) and of politicians who don't care about the landscapes that make where they represent special are amongst the factors adding to their gloom.

But from Norman we can also gain an optimism for our relationship with the remainder of nature:

> Still we climb, higher we climb,
> Through the bracken in the dark combe,
> Through the bilberries and the wild thyme,
>
> Through the mist, through the rain,
> Above the clouds, above the tarn,
> Following the track towards the well remembered cairn.[19]

Whilst this is an early poem of Norman's there is a feeling of wonder and awe at the existence of life, a feeling consistent with the life of the human consciousness that continued throughout his work. Norman remains one of our greatest nature poets, one where natural and human ecologies along with the concern for our need to live in harmony with nature, are part of the same

Footnotes

(18) *Collected Poems* Introduction by Neil Curry p. xxiv.

(19) *Songs of the Island* Collected Poems p. 33 - 34.

whole. He continued the Romantic tradition and despite his death in 1987 his work still carries a fresh and relevant message for our attitude towards nature and for our future within nature.

Duddon Estuary Lighthouse

Norman Nicholson memorial stained glass window, St George's Church, Millom.

APPENDIX 1:

SELECTED BIBLIOGRAPHY
BOOKS BY NORMAN NICHOLSON.

Poetry:

An Anthology of Religious Verse, 1942, London - Penguin.
Selected Poems by John Hall, Keith Douglas and Norman Nicholson, 1943, London - Bale and Staples.
Fiver Rivers, 1944, London - Faber.
Rock Face, 1948, London - Faber.
The Pot Geranium, 1954, London - Faber.
Selected Poems, 1966, London - Faber.
No Star on the Way Back,1967, Manchester - Manchester Institute of Contemporary Arts.
A Local Habitation, 1972, London - Faber.
Stitch and Stone, 1975, Sunderland - Ceolfrith Press.
Cloud on Black Combe, 1975, Hitchin - Cellar Press. (The poem of that title with illustration by Rigby Graham).
The Shadow of Black Combe, 1978, Ashington - Mid-Northumberland Arts Group.
Sea to the West, 1981, London - Faber.
Selected Poems 1940 -1982, 1982, London - Faber.
The Candy Floss Tree: Norman Nicholson, Greda Mayer and Frank Flynn, 1984, Oxford - OUP.
Selected Poems (edited by Neil Curry), 1994, London - Faber & Faber.

Plays:

The Old Man of the Mountains, 1946, London - Faber.
Prophesy to the Wind, 1950, London - Faber.
A Match for the Devil, 1955, London - Faber.
Birth by Drowning, 1960, London - Faber.

Novels:

The Fire of the Lord, 1944, London - Nicholson & Watson.
The Green Shore, 1947, London - Nicholson & Watson.

Literary Criticism and Biography:

Man and Literature, 1943, London - SCM Press

Wordsworth: and Introduction and Selection, 1949, London - Phoenix House.
H.G. Wells, 1950, London - Barker.
William Cowper, 1951, London - Lehmann.
William Cowper, 1960, London - Longmans Green & British Council
A Choice of Cowper's Verse, 1975, London - Faber.

Topographical and Autobiographical:

Cumberland and Westmorland, 1949, London - Hale.
The Lakers, 1955, London - Hale.
Provincial Pleasures, 1959, London - Hale.
Portrait of the Lakes, 1963, London - Hale.
Enjoying it All, 1964, London - Waltham Forest Books (Broadcast Talks)
Greater Lakeland, 1969, London - Hale.
Wednesday Early Closing, 1975, London - Faber.
The Lakes, 1977, London - Hale. Based on the earlier *Portrait of the Lakes*.
The Lake District - an anthology, 1977 London - Hale (and 1978 Penguin).
Ten-yard Panorama, in *Second Nature*, edited by Richard Mabey, 1984, London -Cape

BOOKS FOR OR ABOUT NORMAN NICHOLSON.

Cockley Beck, A Celebration of Lakeland in Winter, 1984, John Pepper, Shaftesbury - Element Books (Chapter 12 is the relevant part but almost the whole book concerns the Duddon valley).
Norman Nicholson, 1973, Philip Gardner, New York - Twyane.
Between Comets, for Norman Nicholson at 70, edited by William Scammell, 1984, Durham - Taxus.
Norman Nicholson, Neil Curry, Carlisle - Northern Lights.
Norman Nicholson The Whispering Poet, 2013, Kathleen Jones, Appleby - The Book Mill

OTHER VOLUMES REFERRED TO.

Walks Around Furness and the Duddon, 1985, Ian Brodie, Clapham - Dalesman.
Mountains of the Mind, Robert Macfarlane, 2003, London - Granta.
Thirlmere and the Birth of the Landscape Conservation Movement, 2012, Ian Brodie, Carlisle - Bookcase.

THE NORMAN NICHOLSON SOCIETY

The internet link is www.normannicholson.org

Wasdale Church.

APPENDIX 2:

NORMAN NICHOLSON'S FOREWORD TO WALKS AROUND FURNESS AND THE DUDDON.

This foreword was written by Norman in late 1984 or early 1985 for a book of walks published by Dalesman in 1985. It is reproduced here because it both returns a long unavailable writing back into print and it tells us how Norman saw the landscape of his home acres late in his life.

'The landscape covered by this book is perhaps the most varied to be found in an area of similar size within, or bordering on, the Lake District National Park. It is mainly, of course, the landscape of the Duddon and its tributaries. Now the Duddon is thought by many people to be the most perfect of all Lakeland dales. It is splendidly individual, self-contained, almost private. It does not peter out at the lower end, as most others do, but keeps its character as a dale right down to the spot where it meets the high tides just below Duddon Bridge.

At this point it opens out into its superb estuary. The river glides through sands and salt-marshes which, on a Bank Holiday, are far lonelier than Scafell. It reaches the sea between the cranes of Barrow Shipyard, on the one side, and, on the other, the grassed over slagbanks, like prehistoric tumuli, which are all that is left of Millom Ironworks. From those slagbanks, or from the old pier, you have what is surely the most glorious inward-looking view from anywhere on the periphery of the Lakes - Black Combe, like a bowler-hat, on the left; the hills of Low Furness, on the right; and, in front, either a fiord at high tide, or an enormous expanse of saltings at low. And beyond all this, there is the great parade of many of the highest fells in the Lakes, from Scafell, Scafell Pike and Bowfell, round to Coniston Old Man, Helvellyn and the distant hills above Haweswater.

The walks in this book explore this country and two of them look further west. One goes round the old sea wall at Hodbarrow, much changed since the mining hollow was flooded giving a new lake the size of Grasmere or Rydal Water. The other goes along the shore from Haverigg to Silecroft, where you cannot forget - as people often do in the central Lakes - that Cumbria is a maritime county. Here the western escarpment of Black Combe, carved steeply by glaciers from Scotland during the Ice Age, drops to a bare, sand-and-shingle beach that looks out to the open sea and the Isle of Man. It is very different from the enclosed landscape of the inner lakes, but it is every bit as Cumbrian.

The whole area, in fact, is the Cumbria of the Cumbrians rather than the Cumbria of the visitors, and those who follow these walks should learn more than they ever would from the promenade at Bowness or the gift shops of Ambleside and Keswick.'
Norman Nicholson

SELECTED INDEX

PEOPLE

PLACES

WILDLIFE

POEMS BY NORMAN NICHOLSON

OTHER HEADINGS

www.ingramcontent.com/pod-product-compliance
Ingram Content Group UK Ltd.
Pitfield, Milton Keynes, MK11 3LW, UK
UKHW020241250726
13967UKWH00001B/494